ASHE Higher Education Report: Volume 37, Number 2
Kelly Ward, Lisa E. Wolf-Wendel, Series Editors

Philanthropy and Fundraising in American Higher Education

Noah D. Drezner

Discover this journal online at
WILEY ONLINE LIBRARY
wileyonlinelibrary.com

71212507/

Philanthropy and Fundraising in American Higher Education
Noah D. Drezner
ASHE Higher Education Report: Volume 37, Number 2
Kelly Ward, Lisa E. Wolf-Wendel, Series Editors

ISSN 1551-6970   electronic ISSN 1554-6306   ISBN 978-1-1181-1033-1

The ASHE Higher Education Report is part of the Jossey-Bass Higher and Adult
Education Series and is published six times a year by Wiley Subscription Services,
Inc., A Wiley Company, at Jossey-Bass, 989 Market Street, San Francisco,
California 94103-1741.

For subscription information, see the Back Issue/Subscription Order Form
in the back of this volume.

CALL FOR PROPOSALS: Prospective authors are strongly encouraged to contact
Kelly Ward (kaward@wsu.edu) or Lisa Wolf-Wendel (lwolf@ku.edu). See "About
the ASHE Higher Education Report Series" in the back of this volume.

Visit the Jossey-Bass Web site at **www.josseybass.com.**

Printed in the United States of America on acid-free recycled paper.

The ASHE Higher Education Report is indexed in CIJE: Current Index to Jour-
nals in Education (ERIC), Current Abstracts (EBSCO), Education Index/Abstracts
(H.W. Wilson), ERIC Database (Education Resources Information Center),
Higher Education Abstracts (Claremont Graduate University), IBR & IBZ: Inter-
national Bibliographies of Periodical Literature (K.G. Saur), and Resources in
Education (ERIC).

Advisory Board

The ASHE Higher Education Report Series is sponsored by the Association for the Study of Higher Education (ASHE), which provides an editorial advisory board of ASHE members.

Contents

Executive Summary

> I have found that among its other benefits, giving liberates the
> soul of the giver.
> —Maya Angelou [National Philanthropic Trust, n.d.]

From gifts of blankets, chickens, and candles to multimillion-dollar gifts and
billion-dollar campaigns, voluntary support of American higher education has
been part of the American ethos since the founding of the colonial colleges.
Although philanthropy and fundraising are part of American postsecondary
education history and essential to most colleges and universities in their ability to offer the level of education, services, and research that we have all
become accustomed to, they are two of the least studied aspects of higher education. This monograph reviews the existing literature and addresses the
impact of philanthropy on American higher education, the theoretical underpinnings and motivations for voluntary support, and a comprehensive look at
the mechanics of fundraising.

   Although private institutions have solicited alumni, friends, foundations,
and corporations for support for centuries, public colleges and universities are
turning more to private giving to meet budgetary demands. As government
support of higher education decreases and the cost to educate a student rises,
the need for philanthropic support to maintain higher education's excellence
and increased access is great. Given this context, the need for more research
on voluntary support is apparent. Currently, the vast majority of philanthropic
literature in higher education is atheoretical and is written almost exclusively
for fundraisers.

Although this atheoretical research offers some guidance for practitioners, the implications are limited by the failure to ground the work in theoretical or conceptual frameworks. As the interdisciplinary academic research on philanthropy has increased, so too has the work in a higher education context. *Philanthropy and Fundraising in American Higher Education* examines the existing literature and proposes future philanthropic and fundraising research that can help fill the theoretical void in the literature, thereby improving future research and fundraising practices in higher education. This monograph covers the major approaches, topics, and theories regarding philanthropy and fundraising for higher education in the United States. Students, practitioners, and researchers are introduced to several key points, among them, the centrality of individual giving in shaping the development and diversity of U.S. higher education, the role of donors as an external force shaping research as well as campus intellectual life and culture, potential critiques of philanthropy's influence, and leading philanthropic theories from the disciplines of psychology, economics, and sociology. Central to this monograph is a discussion of the cultural differences in the definition and manifestation of philanthropy in communities of color and women. As such, I hope that readers will come to understand the significance of the cultural phenomenon of philanthropy as a significant force shaping postsecondary education. This monograph provides the reader with an overview of the basic mechanics of fundraising.

Foreword

Philanthropy and fundraising have probably never been more important to higher education than today. We face a financial perfect storm in higher education. State funding for higher education has declined precipitously in the past two decades, as state governments have come to believe that higher education is a private rather than a public good. This lack of state financing has been exacerbated by the current financial recession, which has led to even more severe financial cutbacks for most publicly funded institutions of higher education. When tax revenues are low, institutions of higher education are less likely to garner as much support as they might in better financial times. State funding, already on the decline, has suddenly decreased even more. The federal government also faces financial declines, and grants as well as other federal sources of financial support for higher education are declining. Endowments have shrunk considerably as the stock market and housing markets have experienced problems. Tuition is as high as it has ever been—making college less affordable for students who want to attend.

At the same time, costs are increasing. Most institutions of higher education are in the do-more-with-less mode. Faculty and staff have not had raises, and some have been furloughed. Yet the costs of higher education continue to rise, including fixed costs for expenses like health insurance, salaries, and the physical plant. So where is this money supposed to come from? For many institutions, the answer is from private donors. Philanthropy is an important part of the equation for helping institutions of higher education, both public and private, weather the financial storm.

When I worked in a development office in graduate school, the first thing I learned was that people give money to things or organizations that do not need it. People want to give money to programs, organizations, and people that are already successful. Those who have, get more. and those who are needy, are less likely to get support. This situation puts institutions of higher education in an interesting predicament: How do we ask for financial support from donors we desperately need without looking desperate? How do we market ourselves as successful to maximize our organizational capacity? Such are the questions asked in this monograph by Noah Drezner, which focuses on individual giving rather than on foundations or other sources of financial support. Through the lens of individual philanthropy, this monograph covers the history of philanthropy, a review of some of the basics of fundraising in higher education, and a discussion of the contemporary theoretical bases underlying giving. It is a useful text for institutional administrators or deans who are worried about future sources of funding and how to maximize individual gifts from donors. It is also useful for researchers and graduate students interested in more theoretical approaches to giving. It does, however, offer an interesting twist to the current obsession of finding the perfect calculus to determine how to maximize individual giving— computing who gives, why they give, and how to get more. This monograph explores, among other topics, how to look more broadly at what philanthropy entails. It talks about how different populations of individuals—white women and people of color, for example—give back to their institutions. This monograph also offers readers some insight into why these populations give, what they give to, and how to maximize their support of your institution.

Other monographs in the series are relevant to this text: *The Entrepreneurial Domains of American Higher Education* by Matthew Mars and Amy Metcalf (Volume 34, Number 5) and *Selling Higher Education: Marketing and Advertising America's Colleges and Universities* by Eric Anctil (Volume 34, Number 2). This monograph by Noah Drezner offers unique perspectives and an appropriate anchor to concerns about philanthropy and where the money will come from to help institutions of higher education weather the rough financial seas ahead.

Lisa E. Wolf-Wendel
Series Editor

Acknowledgments

The idea for this monograph and for including it as part of the ASHE monograph series began when, as a graduate student, I set out on a research career studying philanthropy and fundraising in higher education, only to find the path had many obstacles. The theoretical literature connected to higher education was thin, and the need to understand philanthropic behaviors and philanthropy's effect on colleges and universities was (and continues to be) questioned. That situation has changed in the last few years as more colleagues and students look at private support of higher education and the role of higher education in cultivating new donors and prosocial behaviors beyond the university.

Writing an extended literature review such as this one with the hope that students will gain an appreciation for and an understanding of a topic that I am so passionate about is very rewarding. I very much appreciate the guidance of Lisa Wolf-Wendel and Kelly Ward, the ASHE Higher Education Report series editors, who allowed me to have this opportunity early in my career. I am also grateful to the anonymous reviewers who gave helpful positive and critical feedback that strengthened this manuscript.

I am very fortunate to have a number of students whom I work with formally and informally at the University of Maryland and who have read versions of the manuscript: they have inspired me and have taught me along the way. Thank you to my Ph.D. advisees, Rebecca Villarreal, Steve D. Mobley Jr., Jameel Scott, and Michael Puma, who continually support me in myriad ways. I am excited to see three new philanthropy scholars emerge from my Philanthropy and Fundraising in Higher Education course at Maryland: Kozue Tsunoda, Justin van Fleet, and Jay Garvey. I benefit from their work every time

I read it. Additionally, my colleagues at Maryland provide me with a supportive work environment in which I thrive. I would not have been able to do this work without the continued support of my mentor and close friend, Marybeth Gasman. Marybeth is an inspiration as a scholar, teacher, parent, and a friend. She has supported me and given me opportunities for which I will forever be indebted.

Finally, I cannot imagine my life and my work without the family and friends who support me daily. Thank you to my father, David, for the love, confidence, and support that he continues to give me. My mother, Linda, of blessed memory, whose simple act of giving me a crisp dollar bill every Friday morning to give to *tzedakah* (Hebrew for charity), inspired me in ways I am sure neither of us imagined. I am blessed with an extended family that is always there for support—a special thank you to my Aunt Judy and Uncle Steve Lippard, my cousins Sandra, Josh, and Alex Lippard; Irene and Donald Greenhall and Audrey Greenhall and George Chressanthis. Beyond traditional family, I am privileged to know, learn from, and gain strength from Alan Baldridge, who is not only one of my best friends but is truly a member of my family.

Finally, to the children from whom I gain so much of my inspiration from just being around or hearing stories about: Chloe Epstein; Philip, Matthew, and Christopher Baldridge; Emily and William Chressanthis; and Lucy and Annie Lippard.

This monograph is dedicated to those who inspire me every day through their actions—service and dollars—to make the world a better place.

Published online in Wiley Online Library
(wileyonlinelibrary.com) • DOI: 10.1002/aehe.3702

Introduction

> Philanthropy in America is the public expression of one's social
> and civic values. It barters in financial, human and social capi-
> tal, and empowers common citizens of all financial means to
> take private action on behalf of community good. Philanthropy
> is essential to a vibrant democracy because it brings attention
> to important causes and innovative remedies for which govern-
> ment and business are often less effective. It ensures commu-
> nity ownership of these remedies and guards against total
> dominance of "top down" national policies and majority rule.
>
> —Jessica Chao, 2002/2008, p. 816

ACCORDING TO PHILANTHROPIC STUDIES SCHOLAR Peter
Dobkin Hall, "No single force is more responsible for the emergence of
the modern university in America than giving by individuals and foundations"
(1992, p. 403). This observation is arguably truer today and for the future of
higher education given the current economic crisis. As personal wealth disap-
peared from portfolios, institutional endowments succumbed to the markets as
well. State support of education retreated as tax revenues fell. According to the
annual National Association of College and University Business Officers
(NACUBO) Endowment Study, the average endowment in fiscal year 2008
declined 30 percent. In the first five months of fiscal year 2009, returns fell an
additional 23 percent (National Association of College and University Business Officers, 2009). The conditions of the market led to budget cuts, hiring
freezes, and other substantial reductions in expenditures.

Institutions of higher education, private and public alike, are turning to private giving to meet budgetary demands. As external support of higher education decreases and the cost to educate a student rises, the need for alumni support to maintain higher education's eminence and to increase access heightens. The need for more research on philanthropic giving patterns is apparent. Brittingham and Pezzullo (1990) believe that fundraising is "thinly informed by research" (p. 1). The vast majority of philanthropic literature in higher education is atheoretical (see, for example, Burnett, 1992/2002; Ciconte and Jacob, 2001; Connors, 2001; Dove, 2001; Flanagan, 1999; Greenfield, 2001; Worth, 2002).[1]

Although existing research offers some guidance for practitioners, the implications are limited by the failure to ground the research in theoretical or conceptual frameworks. By failing to ground research and practice in theory, our understanding of people's philanthropic behavior and ways in which practitioners engage and ultimately successfully solicit individual's philanthropic support will ultimately continue to be limited to assumed best practices. Additionally, these best practices do not always include culturally sensitive practices. This monograph examines the philanthropic contributions of individuals through the existing literature and proposes future philanthropic and fundraising research that can help fill the theoretical void in the literature, thereby improving future research and fundraising in higher education.

I have chosen to focus on the philanthropy of individuals rather than that of foundations and corporations, as individual giving to all nonprofits, including higher education, is significantly and consistently higher than other sources. Looking at the most recent data, *Giving USA* (2010) reports that of the $304 billion of philanthropic support given in 2009, 75 percent or $227.4 billion came from living donors and an additional $24 billion was given through bequests of individuals who had passed away. Additionally, the power of individual philanthropy is even stronger when looking at foundations. Family foundations, whose giving ultimately comes from individuals but is used as a mechanism for tax incentives, account for an additional $15.4 billion. Therefore, philanthropic giving from individuals totaled $267 billion or 88 percent of voluntary support in 2009. The remaining 12 percent came from foundations (nonfamily and noncorporate—$23 billion or 7.5 percent) and corporations (including corporate foundations—$14 billion or 4.6 percent). More specific to higher education, the 2010 Voluntary Support of Education survey found that in 2009, $27.85 billion was given by all sources. Of that amount, $7.13 billion (25.6 percent) was donated by alumni and an additional $5 billion (17.9 percent) came from non-alumni individuals. Thus, individuals accounted for 43.5 percent of giving to higher education. The remaining voluntary support came from foundations ($8.24 billion, 29.6 percent), corporations ($4.62 billion, 16.6 percent), organizations ($2.55 billion, 9.1 percent), and religious organizations ($33 million, 1.2 percent).

Therefore, this monograph covers the major approaches, topics, and theories regarding philanthropy and fundraising from individuals to postsecondary education in the United States. Students, practitioners, and researchers are introduced to several key points, among them the centrality of private giving in shaping the development and diversity of U.S. higher education; the role of donors as an external force shaping research, campus intellectual life, and culture; the role of philanthropy in access; and leading philanthropic theories from the disciplines of psychology, sociology, and economics. As such, it is my hope that readers will attain an understanding of the cultural phenomenon of philanthropy as a significant force shaping postsecondary education.

A greater understanding of philanthropy in the higher education setting is critical because of the increased reliance on voluntary giving at all colleges and universities, the recent economic downturn, and the imminent "great wealth transfer," for which it is thought that $6 trillion will likely be given to nonprofit organizations, including higher education, over the next fifty-five years (Schervish and Havens, 1998). (A more detailed discussion of the great wealth transfer appears later in this chapter.) Plummeting endowments, retrenchment of state appropriations, and the possibilities of engaging a broader range of donors (improving outreach to women, communities of color, and the LGBTQQI[2] populations) make understanding the theories, motivations, dynamics, and ethics of philanthropy even more important. This monograph aims to do just that.

Although philanthropy has been part of American higher education since its inception, the study of its impact on academe is much more recent. Walton and Gasman (2008) contend that "because the study of philanthropy is complex, value-laden, and burdened by issues of the unequal distribution of power in society, scholars have been reticent about the topic" (p. xxiii). Access to data sources and archival materials also made scholarly inquiry difficult.

According to Hall (1992), many scholars avoided the study of philanthropy "because it tended to lead them [toward] the kinds of essentially political concerns with wealth and power that were unlikely to enhance their career prospects" (p. 403). The 1975 report of the Commission on Private Philanthropy and Public Needs—often referred to as the Filer Commission after the chairman of the commission—and the founding of the Independent Sector in 1980 led to a new interest in the study of the nonprofit sector and its effect on civic engagement and the shaping of the United States civic, cultural, and intellectual institutions.

The Independent Sector in many ways professionalized the nonprofit sector. The Independent Sector is a consortium of leaders from nonprofits, foundations, and corporate giving programs that are "committed to advancing the common good in America and around the world" through creating and supporting "a just and inclusive society and a healthy democracy of active citizens, effective institutions, and vibrant communities" (Independent Sector, 2011). Over the past thirty years, the Independent Sector has sponsored research on philanthropy and the nonprofit sector, supported the creation and implementation of public policies in the interest of nonprofits, and supported the professional development of nonprofits' staffs, boards, and volunteers.

Through the work of the Filer Commission and the early work of the Independent Sector, scholarship on philanthropy and nonprofits began to gain more acceptance in the 1980s. According to *The Chronicle of Higher Education,* however, "scholars aren't being named to distinguished professorships in the history of charitable giving, and academic departments don't appear to be designing positions for specialists in the subject" (Desruisseaux, 1985, p. 18). This situation is beginning to change with the establishment of both graduate and undergraduate programs in philanthropic studies in the last few years.

To lay a framework of understanding for this monograph, I begin with an overview of philanthropy and fundraising concepts, explaining the day-to-day operations of advancement practitioners and different strategies employed to seek voluntary funds to higher education. The operations and functional areas of the annual fund, comprehensive campaigns, and planned giving are explored. This chapter also discusses the important role voluntary support has had on contemporary American higher education.

The Concepts and Mechanics of Fundraising

Tomas Broce wrote that "fund raising as a professional process is best understood when considered in the broader process. . . . [It] encompasses the entire operation from goal identification to gift solicitation" (1986, p. 27). As such, to understand the effect of philanthropy by individuals on American higher education, it is best to understand the fundraising processes employed to solicit those gifts.

As discussed in more detail in the next chapter, fundraising has been part of American higher education since the founding of Harvard, but it was not done comprehensively and in a concerted manner. Fundraising as an organized venture is much more recent. At first, many institutions hired outside fundraising firms (many for-profit corporations and partnerships) to handle campaigns and even their annual solicitations. For example, Harvard hired John Price Jones in 1919 to administer its first full-fledged organized campaign that asked "regular" alumni for their support (Cutlip, 1965). At historically black colleges and universities, fundraising firms were used through the 1970s (Gasman and Drezner, 2008, 2009, 2010). Today, most universities handle all their fundraising in-house.

These in-house fundraising offices are often called "development offices" but more recently have been named "institutional advancement offices." They are organized in numerous ways. Some are centralized so that all fundraising is handled by the central administration, while others are decentralized so that each college, school, or center has its own development office and is organized centrally for coordination and some shared costs. Often universities use a hybrid approach (Worth, 2002, 2010).

However advancement offices are organized, the principles of fundraising are the same. Gifts are categorized in two main ways: (1) unrestricted giving, the most coveted, where funds can be used at the university's discretion, often referred to as "where the money is needed most," and (2) restricted gifts, where the donor indicates, usually through a legal document called a "gift agreement," how the gifts should be used. Larger restricted gifts are often invested in the institution's endowment, providing funds to support the donor's wishes in perpetuity. In addition to these types of gifts, some current use gifts—those donations that are to be spent the fiscal year they are received—might have some minimal restrictions placed on them by the donor. These "semiunrestricted gifts" might be designated to a specific department but the university decides how they are spent in the department. These gifts can be used for scholarships, faculty chairs, care and maintenance of new or existing university facilities, or almost anything that a university and donor agree upon. Later in this chapter is a brief explanation of how endowments work. First, however, is an introduction to the traditional means in which money is raised—annual funds, campaigns, and planned giving instruments. A more detailed discussion of these fundraising methods is found in Appendix A.

Annual Funds

The annual fund is one of the basic building blocks of any fundraising enterprise. As the name suggests, it is typically an annual appeal. Most annual funds have multiple objectives. First, and perhaps foremost, annual funds at most colleges and universities provide operating support through unrestricted gifts (Schroeder, 2002). Many institutions, however, now allow donors to place some restrictions on their annual fund gifts. For example, donors may designate their gifts for a specific college or school, academic department, or student affairs office. This less-traditional approach to unrestricted giving was established in response to donors' requesting and requiring more control in determining how their funds are used. By allowing these semiunrestricted gifts, institutions retain a fair amount of control over where the dollars can be spent.

A second, and perhaps equally important, role of the annual fund is to broaden institutional support by acquiring new donors through their regular solicitation. Another role of the annual fund is to cultivate and increase commitments of previous donors. These "upgrades," as they are known in development offices, are not just to increase the college's or university's income but are asked for with the hope of moving the donor toward higher levels of annual giving, major gifts, and future planned giving (Lindahl, 2009;

Schroeder, 2002). In other words, the annual fund in essence nurtures tomorrow's major donors by creating an annual habit of philanthropy.

This annual habit of philanthropy is supported by continuity theory, which, according to Atchley (1989), establishes patterns that are likely to be followed in the future. Others have used Atchley's theory to explain continual giving in a philanthropic context (Lindahl and Winship, 1992; Okunade and Justice, 1991; Piliavin and Charng, 1990). Lindahl and Winship (1992) and Okunade and Justice (1991) found that past giving behaviors are positively correlated with current and future giving practices. Cascione (2003) referred to it as reinforcement theory in the context of higher education. A more detailed discussion of these theories is found in "What Guides the Study of Philanthropy and Fundraising?"

Campaigns

Building off the regular support of individuals through the annual fund, institutions use campaigns to excite donors and engage them in larger gifts to their college or university. Fundraising campaigns are becoming more popular in American higher education. At one time they were reserved for special purposes such as developing a new building (Worth, 2010). These campaigns for brick and mortar are typically called "capital campaigns," but today more institutions are running "comprehensive campaigns" that include fundraising priorities for improvements to their physical plant, endowment building, and even annual giving (Worth, 2010). The endowment portions of campaigns can be designated for scholarships, faculty chairs, programming, or any other priority the university might designate.

Campaigns today are often continuous. As one ends, another one begins. Comprehensive campaigns typically last between seven and ten years, with multiple phases. McGoldrick and Robell (2002) and Worth (2010) have broken down the typical campaign as follows: (1) precampaign (six to eighteen months), in which feasibility studies are often completed by professional fundraising consultants external to the college or university; (2) campaign planning (three to six months), in which priorities are identified, some goals are set, and campaign leadership is identified; (3) nucleus fund or quiet phase (one to two years), during which planning continues and volunteer campaign leaders are brought on board and solicited for lead gifts (typically all gifts to the institution are counted at this point although the campaign has not yet been publicly announced); and (4) the public phase (three to five years), during which the campaign is officially kicked off.

According to McGoldrick and Robell (2002), institutions should have already raised between 40 to 50 percent of their goal at the official announcement of the campaign. With the increased number of billion-dollar campaigns, however, this number has dropped to closer to 33 percent of the goal (Worth, 2010). As the campaign progresses, it typically reaches a point where the excitement wears off, referred to as a "plateau of fatigue." Excitement tends to be rejuvenated in the home stretch of a successful campaign, as institution, donors, and alumni are able to celebrate the closing (McGoldrick and Robell, 2002).

During comprehensive campaigns, all donors are asked to make "stretch gifts" to the institution, although campaign goals have already been built around large lead gifts. David Dunlop (2002), a former development officer at Cornell University and often thought of as one of leading major gift officers in the nation, once observed that 80 percent of campaign goals were given by 20 percent of donors. He called this phenomenon the 80/20 rule. As campaign goals have grown larger and larger and wealth disparities have grown as well (Conley, 2000), the 80/20 rule has become the 90/10 or even the 95/5 rule. Dunlop (2002), noting the significance of this change, observed that prospective donors might be asked, based on financial capacity and interest, to give between five to twenty times their regular giving during a comprehensive campaign. Calling it a "special gift," Dunlop further denoted the potential for gifts 500 to 1,000 times larger as "transformational gifts," typically given as planned gifts.

Planned Giving

Planned gifts are often referred to as the "ultimate gift," as they are typically larger gifts that are planned in advance of the donor's passing away (Sapp and Kimball, 2002). A number of different charitable instruments are available to donors, their families, and the institution to join in agreement with one another. These options are complex and often require a lawyer or other person very knowledgeable in current IRS regulations and tax law working with both the institution and donor or the donor's family. Although the tax savings can be significant for wealthy individuals, financial benefits alone rarely motivate the gift. The practical considerations of simplifying one's life, relinquishing asset management, or maintaining control of income often are important considerations of potential planned giving donors (Spears, 2001). Five types of instruments are the most popular: (1) charitable gift annuities; (2) charitable remainder trusts; (3) charitable lead trusts; (4) pooled income funds; and (5) deferred gifts or bequests. A detailed discussion of these instruments is in Appendix A.

Understanding How Endowments Work

Many of the largest donations to higher education through campaigns and mechanisms such as planned gifts are designated to be placed in institutional endowments. An institutional endowment can be viewed as the investment portfolio of the college or university. Endowment gifts often are given to universities with stipulations for their use. Most endowed gifts are given to support student scholarships or faculty salaries and research through endowed professorships or chairs. Besides scholarships and faculty salaries, institutions typically also use endowments to cover the costs of maintaining and upgrading the physical plant. Often when raising money for a new capital project such as a building, the fundraising goal includes the cost of construction and the creation of an endowment to cover the maintenance and upkeep of the new building. Nevertheless, endowments can be created to support any portion of the university when a donor and university agree.

Endowed gifts are different from "regular" current use gifts in that the gift is invested in a university portfolio as principal that must remain intact in perpetuity. Only a portion of the annual returns on the investment are spent on the designated cause. Thus, endowed gifts have an impact on the university and the cause designated in perpetuity rather than during a short time period as current use gifts are allocated. Gifts to an endowment are typically from individual donors, as foundations usually give their gifts for current uses (Worth, 2002). Most university endowment gifts are given by alumni to support their alma mater (Massy, 1990; Council for Aid to Education, 2010).

The governing board of the college or university oversees the endowment, and typically a team of professional financial officers manages it. Institutions on average use 4 to 6 percent of the endowment's assets on the designated uses, called the spending rate. Each college or university sets its own spending rate, often based on the past five years of investment returns (Massy, 1990). The spending rate is set to prevent diminishing the principal of the original gift but also allows for the growth of the endowment through the continual reinvestment of a portion of the annual investment returns. The reinvested portion of the returns allows for a regular growth in the endowment, regardless of new investment, and protects future spending from inflation and recessions. Historically, endowment performance follows the stock markets and gains 10 to 11 percent annually. With the average spending rate around 5 percent, the remaining 5 to 6 percent is reinvested. Inflation is typically 3 percent during periods of economic growth; therefore, the remaining 2 to 3 percent of reinvestment allows for continued growth in spending.

The ways in which individual donors are able to financially support higher education are vast and often complex. As development offices become more sophisticated and try to engage many more individuals in giving, these mechanisms to increase participation have and will continue to evolve. Having a better understanding of the mechanics and means in which colleges and universities solicit support, the following will now explore the effects these fundraising techniques have had on higher education.

Significance of Contemporary Philanthropy in Higher Education

A number of annual reports are available on philanthropic giving. For more than fifty years, *Giving USA* has informed scholars and practitioners alike about national donation trends to the entire third sector. The Voluntary Support of Education survey looks specifically at giving to postsecondary education. Participation in the survey is not required; therefore, it is incomplete.

According to *Giving USA,* individuals are responsible for the majority of giving to colleges and universities. Of these donors, the majority are alumni of the institution that they support. As such, alumni are at the core of college and university advancement processes. Not only do these contributions support the day-to-day operations of an institution, but they also demonstrate to other potential outside donors such as foundations and corporations that the alumni and alumnae are committed to the future success of the institution.

As competition has increased for dollars among all postsecondary institutions, philanthropic support of education—and specifically higher education—has escalated immensely. In fact, since 1965 giving to all aspects of education increased from $2.01 billion (in constant dollars) to $40.01 billion in 2009, an increase of 1,891 percent (*Giving USA*, 2010).

Although this increase is substantial, it should be noted that in the current economic downturn, giving to education declined 5.4 percent in 2008 and 3.6 percent in 2009, accounting for an 8.8 percent drop from 2007 giving levels (*Giving USA*, 2010). But even during the tough economy, private support of education has increased substantially and is at near-record levels.

According to *Giving USA* (2010), donors gave $303.75 billion to qualified nonprofit organizations in 2009. Religious organizations received the greatest percentage of private monies (33 percent), while all levels of education received the second greatest percentage (13 percent). Exhibit 1 indicates all of the areas of giving identified in the *Giving USA* study.

Higher education received the greatest support of all educational levels (Exhibit 2). The 2002 edition of *Giving USA* is the most recent year that educational philanthropy was broken down by organizational type.

The dollars raised and requested are at all-time highs, even when accounting for inflation. As of June 2010, seventy-five campaigns with goals of more than $1 billion had been announced or completed at institutions in the United States. Of those seventy-five campaigns, forty-nine were successfully completed and in fact exceeded their original goals. The remaining twenty-six are currently in the public phase of their campaign. Further, of the seventy-five campaigns, twelve are at institutions that had previously completed a billion-dollar-plus campaign (Grenzebach Glier & Associates, 2010; Lopez-Rivera, 2010). The billion-dollar-plus campaigns together have a combined goal of raising $112.6 billion and as of this writing have raised a combined total of $113.6 billion. The amount raised is higher than the stated goals because all the campaigns that were active during the late 1990s and early 2000s closed significantly above

EXHIBIT 1

Uses of Charitable Giving in 2009

Type of Recipient Organization	Amount ($ Billions)	Percent
Religion	100.95	33
Education	**40.01**	**13**
Foundations (estimate)	31.00	10
Unallocated Giving	28.59	10
Human Services	27.08	9
Public-Society Benefit	22.77	8
Health	22.46	7
Arts, Culture, and Humanities	12.34	4
International Affairs	8.89	3
Environment/Animals	6.15	2
Foundation Gifts to Individuals	3.51	1
Total	303.75	100

Source: Giving USA, 2010.

EXHIBIT 2

Charitable Contributions to Education in 2002

Type of Educational Organization	Percent
U.S. Higher Education	62
K–12 Education	8
Scholarship	8
Other	8
International Higher Education	7
Donor-Advised Funds	5
Libraries	2
Approximate Total	100

Source: American Association of Fundraising Counsel, 2003, p. 120.

their original goals. Cornell University is currently in the largest campaign ever announced, seeking to raise $4 billion by the end of 2011.

Along with increased competition for funds and larger campaign goals, the higher education fundraising sector has seen the growth of megagifts from individual donors, beginning in the 1990s with the dot-com boom on the West

Coast. For example, in 1999 the Bill and Melinda Gates Foundation gave $1 billion in support of scholarships for African American, Latino, and Native American students. This donation is managed by the United Negro College Fund (UNCF). In addition, in 2001 Stanford received the largest donation ever to a single institution—$400 million—from the Hewlett-Packard Foundation (Worth, 2002). As mentioned before, such gifts narrow the fundraising pyramid, "with a higher percentage of total support coming from fewer and fewer gifts at the very top" (p. 33). According to a 1999 survey by the Council for the Advancement and Support of Education, 80 percent of donations came from the top 10 percent of the nation's donors. Moreover, 57 percent of gifts to higher education come from the top 1 percent of donors (Worth, 2002).

The Great Wealth Transfer

Giving to education will likely only rise in the future. Havens and Schervish noted that over the next fifty-five years, America will experience a "great wealth transfer" wherein $41 trillion will likely be passed from one generation to the next through bequests, philanthropy, and taxes. A conservative estimate by Havens and Schervish is that of the great wealth transfer, 15 percent, or $6 trillion, will be given to nonprofit organizations (Havens and Schervish, 1999, 2003).

It is important to note that Havens and Schervish conducted their study in 1999 before the Bush tax cuts were enacted in 2001 and 2003 and recently renewed in 2010. These tax cuts eliminated estate taxes and the tax advantage for charitable giving at death. It is unclear how the $6 trillion estimate will be affected by the tax cuts if they are adopted permanently (Drezner, 2006). Joulfaian (2000), from the U.S. Treasury Department, found that the estate tax deduction given for charitable bequests is "budget efficient"; that is, it encourages giving at a rate higher than the revenue lost by the government. Joulfaian estimates in the absence of the estate tax, charitable bequests might decline by 12 percent. But Butler (2001), vice president of domestic and economic policy studies at the Heritage Foundation, a conservative think tank, uses Milton Friedman's permanent income/overlapping generations theory to refute Joulfaian. Butler contends that according to Friedman's theory, a person's residual wealth (after heirs are taken care of) goes to philanthropic causes and therefore, he believes, eliminating the estate tax charitable bequests will increase as the after-tax cost of planned contributions to heirs would be reduced (Butler, 2001).

Steinberg, Wilhelm, Rooney, and Brown (2002), in a study at the Center on Philanthropy using the Philanthropy Panel Study from the larger Panel Study of Income Dynamics, painted a bleak picture for the great wealth transfer. They found "that the elasticity of giving from non-inherited wealth is much greater than from inherited wealth . . . although inherited wealth creates a higher marginal propensity to donate" (p. 1). In other words, these authors agreed with Avery (1994) that those who make money are far more generous than those who inherit it, even though those who inherit wealth do increase their overall giving with their newly found disposable income. Using the marginal propensity to give (evaluated at the mean), the 2002 study found that those who inherit wealth "will be 3.2 times less generous with the money they received" than their benefactors (Steinberg, Wilhelm, Rooney, and Brown, 2002, p. 15). Therefore, as the wealth transfer continues, annual giving to nonprofits might fall (Steinberg, Wilhelm, Rooney, and Brown, 2002).

Individuals' voluntary support to American higher education is vast. Considering the $113.6 billion raised in the last two decades by just sixty-three higher education institutions (through billion-dollar-plus campaigns) and the potential of approximately $78 billion being given to education through the great wealth transfer,[3] the importance of understanding the phenomenon of individual voluntary support of higher education is clear. Through the rest of the monograph, it is the author's hope that readers will understand philanthropy and fundraising more and perhaps some readers will choose to research the topic.

An Organizational Guide to the Rest of the Monograph

This monograph is organized into nine chapters. The next chapter provides examples that show how individual philanthropy has influenced American higher education. The chapter is limited by space, for an entire monograph (or more) could be devoted to the history of philanthropy's influence on American higher education. In 1973 the Council for Financial Aid to Education declared that American higher education was "elevate[d] to a position of excellence" by philanthropy (p. 9). The chapter discusses how private support affects what is taught and researched and who gained access to higher education.

The following chapter asks "who is philanthropic?" For the longest time, philanthropy was associated with "a relatively small number of White families and individuals [men] who enjoyed access to education, owned major businesses, held leadership positions in government, dominated the professions, and inherited wealth" (Council on Foundations, 1999, p. 7). Therefore, the chapter explores the emerging literature on the philanthropic traditions of groups that have historically been seen as "takers" but actually have long been civically responsible citizens and residents who "give back." The following chapter looks at women's giving.

"What Guides the Study of Philanthropy and Fundraising?" explores the theoretical underpinnings, interpretive frameworks, and motivations for philanthropic action. The chapter reviews the most prominent theories from the disciplines of economics, psychology, and sociology in the philanthropic literature as applied to higher education. Fundraisers often do not rely on theory to guide their practice, and most fundraising literature is written for practitioners offering supposedly "best" practices, often not grounded in theory (Brittingham and Pezzullo, 1989; Carbone, 1986; Kelly, 1991). Further understanding donors' motivations and successful fundraising strategies from a theoretical standpoint, philanthropy and fundraising research allows practitioners to enhance their development programs, expanding them to new prospect pools by better understanding how donors choose to participate.

"Engaging Students and Young Alumni" looks at the process of engaging these groups in prosocial behavior. The involvement of undergraduate students in alumni and fundraising activities at institutions creates a strong foundation for active alumni support after graduation. The chapter looks at the scholarship that investigates how institutions might instill a culture of giving among their students, their future alumni donors. The importance of engaging students in fundraising programs and even as donors early in their careers is explored.

Philanthropy has the power to open doors of opportunity and save and enrich lives. But it also involves the potential for harm and the need for critique. The actions, motives, and outcomes of individual, foundation, and corporate philanthropy are all subject to evaluation. "Who Gives?" looks critically at philanthropy, in particular giving to higher education.

With the creation of Ph.D. and bachelor's degree programs in philanthropic studies and with more researchers looking at philanthropy from a critical perspective, the research is expanding. The final chapter recommends future research and practice. Two appendices conclude the monograph, the first covering the mechanics of fundraising and the second resources for philanthropic research.

The Influence of Philanthropy on American Higher Education

> The raising of extraordinarily large sums of money, given voluntarily and freely by millions of our fellow Americans, is a unique American tradition. . . . Philanthropy, charity, giving voluntarily and freely. . . . Call it what you like, but it is truly a jewel of an American tradition.
>
> —John F. Kennedy [National Philanthropic Trust, n.d.]

AMERICANS' GIVING HAS SHAPED HIGHER EDUCATION. In fact, Hall suggested that "no single force is more responsible for the emergence of the modern university in America than giving by individuals and foundations" (1992, p. 403). Further, the Council for Aid to Education (1973) declared that American higher education was elevated "to a position of excellence" by philanthropy (p. 9). To understand the contemporary phenomenon of philanthropic giving toward higher education, it is best to have an understanding of how past giving has shaped postsecondary education. In the space provided in this monograph, it simply is impossible to provide a comprehensive and detailed history of philanthropy and fundraising toward higher education. As such, this chapter simply highlights some of the significant moments of the past 375 years. Rather than provide a traditional chronological telling of a history of philanthropic giving to American higher education, the chapter is structured by a number of themes: (1) British support in the colonies; (2) colonial support; (3) individual donor influence, including the creation of new colleges; (4) issues of donor control; and (5) the rise of alumni giving.

British Support for the Creation of American Higher Education

From John Harvard's 1638 bequest to the colonies' first college to present-day multibillion dollar campaigns at private and public institutions throughout the country, fundraising has been an important aspect of American higher education. The founding of higher education in British colonies was supported mostly through gifts coming from England. In *New England's First Fruits* (1643/2004), a Harvard College document that many consider the first higher education fundraising brochure, the author describes citizens who "longed . . . to advance learning and perpetuate it to prosperity" through gifts to education. Although, according to Cutlip (1965), systematic and organized fundraising is a phenomenon of the American twentieth century, philanthropic endeavors toward higher education were a part of colonial America by means of England. The early American economy was not able to support its own charitable activities to found and support colleges (Ashcraft, 1995; Meuth, 1992). Sustaining the academy, through large donations, was left to the Old World, mostly through donations from Britain: "Individual benevolence was nonetheless in the English tradition, and the colonial colleges therefore naturally looked to it for sustenance. At first, England itself was the only reliable source of significant philanthropy. The Englishmen John Harvard and Elihu Yale, while not the founders of the colleges that took their names, were the first substantial private benefactors of collegiate education in New England" (Rudolph, 1962, p. 178). The setting of Yale College provides a good example of this kind of early philanthropy. Jeremiah Dummer, a Harvard College alumnus, played an important role in the founding and support of Yale, then known as the Collegiate College in New Haven. Dummer was appointed the colonial agent for Massachusetts and Connecticut. In this role, he began to solicit donations for Collegiate College, eventually securing donations from the British philanthropist Elihu Yale. In trying to convince Yale to support the college that would eventually bear his name, Dummer wrote to Yale "that the business of good men is to spread religion and learning among mankind" (Kelley, 1974, p. 24). Yale eventually agreed to aid the college.

In 1718 the school was renamed Yale College in gratitude for the support. Elihu Yale's gift was small by today's standards. He donated the proceeds of nine bales of hay, 417 books, and a portrait of King George I (Kelley, 1974). Although many other people have given to Yale and at higher amounts, Elihu Yale was in the right place at the right time.

The colonial colleges—Harvard, William and Mary, Yale, Dartmouth, Brown, Columbia, Rutgers, Princeton, Pennsylvania, and Delaware—received many smaller gifts than Yale's from donors who understood the importance of higher education. "The [colonial] colleges were . . . saved by the development of widespread popular interest in higher education, interest intense enough to impel thousands of individuals, both in America and in the British Isles, to make cash gifts aggregating a very considerable amount" (Cutlip, 1965, p. 5). Historians suggest that although American higher education and the private support of it have roots in Europe, it was transformed into an American tradition quickly after its arrival in the colonies (Curti and Nash, 1965; Rudolph, 1962; Walton, 2008).

Support from the American Colonies

The American Revolution ended the relationship between the colonial colleges and the British educational philanthropists such as John Harvard and Elihu Yale. Many of the donations to the colleges from colonists were given without any restrictions on how they could be used. Rather than invested for the future in endowments, institutions spent the gifts to build buildings, buy books, offer scholarships, and pay salaries. The purpose of these gifts was not only to further academic learning but also to educate those who attended in the region. The original small gifts of candles, blankets, and chickens to support the newly formed colonial colleges showed that the colonists believed that higher education was a public good even by those with modest means. Curti and Nash (1965) realized that these gifts were very significant to the future of educational fundraising not because of their size—in fact, they were small—but because "higher education and its philanthropic support were planted as ideas and actualities in American soil" (p. 41).

Those Colonial colleges that developed cultures of philanthropy since their inception, however, were still successful at raising funds and furthering the culture of philanthropic giving toward their institutions. Even with the limited resources for education, the nineteenth century was a period of increased growth in higher education. The most successful colleges were those that were the most accomplished in fundraising (Rudolph, 1962). The need for and importance of external support for American higher education even made it into university songs and hymns. The first verse of the Harvard Hymn, written by James Bradstreet Greenough, Harvard class of 1856, and sung at every commencement in Latin says: *"Deus omnium creator, rerum mundi moderator, crescat cuius es fundator nostra universita . . . largiantur donatores benepartas copias,"* which translated is, "God, the creator of everything, controller of the things of this world, may that of which you are the founder grow, our university. . . . may the donors supply their well-gotten abundance" (Harvard, n.d.). With the donors' supply of their "well-gotten abundance," however, comes immediate questions of influence by donors.

Influence of Individual Donors

Along with gifts often comes the expectation of influence from the donors. Higher education and its principles of shared governance and academic freedom perhaps complicate to what extent this level of influence is appropriate. In the next few sections the author shares some examples of donor influence and how it has shaped American higher education.

Endowed Chairs

From nearly the beginning of individual giving to American higher education, donors have influenced decision making at the institutions they support. Beginning in the eighteenth century, donors realized that they could "push" their influence onto colleges through their money. One example is Thomas Hollis. Hollis funded an endowed chair in divinity at Harvard in 1721. An endowed chair is a faculty position permanently funded by a gift invested in the institutional endowment. Although it is common for universities now, the Hollis Professor of Divinity was the first endowed chair known to exist in

American higher education. Through his donation, Hollis sought to foster institutional change and solidify the institution's commitment to the study of religion.

Interestingly, Hollis, a Baptist, stipulated that Harvard may not have a specific doctrinal requirement of the professor appointed to the position. He specified, however, that the professor should be "of solid learning in divinity, of sound, or orthodox principles, one well gifted to teach, of a sober and pious life, and of a grave conversation" (Bradford, 1837, p. 350). Hollis's hope to ensure the continued study of religion at Harvard might not have occurred without the creation of the endowed chair. In the 1830s, Harvard was in difficult financial times and then-Harvard president Josiah Quincy III decided that the institution should move away from the teaching of religion (Shoemaker, 2008). Quincy thought that the original Hollis endowment was exhausted in the financial troubles (Morison, 1986). When he realized it was not the case, the Hollis chair was reinstated as part of the Harvard Divinity School, thereby reintroducing the study of religion to Harvard.

Donors' influence has affected not only aspects of a particular institution but also the creation of new types of institutions. The next three sections explore the creation of women's, black, and teacher's colleges from philanthropic donations and their donors' influence.

The Creation of Women's Colleges

Donors' influence was also part of the establishment of women's colleges. For example, Smith College was founded as a result of a bequest of Sophia Smith. The "Last Will and Testament of Miss Sophia Smith" was not completed until March 1870—only three months before she died. The final version of her will supported "the establishment and maintenance of an Institution for the higher education of young women, with the design to furnish for my own sex means and facilities for education equal to those which are afforded now in our Colleges to young men." The will went on, "It is my opinion that by the education of women, what are called their 'wrongs' will be redressed, their wages adjusted, their weight of influence in reforming the evils of society will be greatly increased, as teachers, as writers, as mothers, as members of society, their power for good will be incalculably enlarged." As a result, Smith College was chartered in 1871 and opened in 1875, giving women access to higher education in a way that they never had before.

The Creation of Black Colleges

Similar to the establishment of women's colleges to ensure the equal education of both genders, philanthropy allowed for the creation of black colleges in the South after the Civil War. Both whites and blacks supported the creation of these institutions. Given the historic racism in the United States, the philanthropic support for the creation of black colleges by whites is perhaps more complicated—in terms of motivation—than the creation of women's colleges by women and teacher's colleges by educators.

Gasman and Drezner (2009) pointed out that "within the uneven and generally out-of-date literature on the history of philanthropy and fundraising in higher education, there has been much attention paid to white industrial philanthropists and their support of black colleges during the late 19th and early 20th century" (p. 468). Multiple scholarly views exist on the actions of these donors. Some contend these wealthy businessmen supported black education as a means of benevolence (Curti and Nash, 1965; Jencks and Riesman, 1967; Sowell, 1972). For example, Jencks and Riesman (1967) found that the white industrial philanthropists who supported the establishment of black colleges were altruistic and were not motivated by their own personal monetary gains. "Rather than assuming a Machiavellian plot to support 'Uncle Toms' like Booker T. Washington against 'militants' like W.E.B. DuBois, we would argue that the Northern whites who backed private colleges for Negroes were moved by genuinely philanthropic motives" (Jencks and Riesman, 1967, p. 16). Revisionist scholars observe efforts of these philanthropists as more of a self-serving business move that was aimed at controlling the southern labor market (Anderson, 1988; Lewis, 1994; Watkins, 2001). Anderson (1988) contended that the industrial philanthropist's "philosophy [was] that higher education ought to direct black boys and girls to places in life that were congruent with the South's racial caste system, as opposed to providing them with knowledge and experiences that created a wide, if not unlimited, range of social and economic possibilities" (p. 248). Finally, Anderson and Moss (1999) argued a more nuanced and neutral view of these donors, drawing on the deep religious commitments of the philanthropists and how beliefs influenced their capitalist mentalities. Anderson and Moss (1999) acknowledged that although northern philanthropists did accede to the South's caste system, they argued that the "philanthropists had a vision of race relations (and black potential) that was significantly different from the ideas of the South's white majority" (p. 11). Many scholars have explored the individual industrial philanthropist's involvement in the support of black colleges through the gifts of philanthropists such as Andrew Carnegie, George Foster Peabody, John D. Rockefeller Sr., and Julius Rosenwald (Ascoli, 2006; Chernow, 2004; Dalzell and Dalzell, 2007; Nasaw, 2006). Others have examined the actions of organizations such as the Southern Education Foundation and the General Education Board on behalf of black colleges, often looking critically at their efforts and pointing to notions of paternalism and control (Anderson, 1988; Anderson and Moss, 1999; Lewis, 1994; Watkins, 2001). White industrial philanthropists have made significant contributions to the establishment of black colleges; however, blacks themselves have long been donors as well (see the following chapter for a further discussion of black individuals' support of black colleges).

The Creation of Teachers Colleges

With the influence of Thomas Hollis on what was taught and researched at Harvard and the creation of colleges specifically for the education of women and blacks, philanthropists have influenced how research and practice are aligned. For example, donors influenced the standards and teacher preparation programs at many schools of education around the country through the establishment of Teachers College in 1887. Many of these standards are still practiced and taught today. Philanthropist Grace Hoadley Dodge and philosopher Nicholas Murray Butler founded Teachers College, now part of Columbia University, to ensure that those teaching students, particularly the poor, in New York were able to teach with a humanitarian concern to help others and with an understanding of human development (Walton, 2000). Their establishment of Teachers College is significant in that donors influenced not only what was being taught but also the way that teachers practiced as professionals. The next section addresses issues when donors' influence is perhaps too strong.

Issues of Donors' Control

Later in the twentieth century, we began to see a new level of influence by individual donors that crossed over into what is commonly referred to as "donor control issues." In the late 1920s, Linda Miller, the widow of a New York businessman, established an endowed chair in memory of her recently deceased husband. The Nathan L. Miller Professor of Jewish History, Literature and Institutions at Columbia University first established an academic home for Jewish studies in academe. This gift differed from earlier endowed chairs in that Mrs. Miller wanted to select who would hold the chair, while Columbia wanted to protect the faculty hiring process from donors' influence. Salo Baron was appointed in 1929 without the input of the chair's benefactor (Ritterband and Wechsler, 1994). Understanding this level of influence raises important questions for universities today: How much power do we give donors, and when do we say "no" to a gift, given the donor's requirements? (See "Who Gives?" later in this monograph.)

Giving as a Collective: Alumni Giving and the Beginning of Systematic Solicitation

Although it is clear from the examples above that individual donors have significantly influenced American higher education, it is important to note the impact of the collective. Philanthropy that up until the turn of the twentieth century was reserved for and expected only from the wealthiest was then solicited from alumni of different means. With Harvard's class of 1881 gift of $113,777 in 1906, the idea of class gifts became popular (Curti and Nash, 1965). The regular solicitation of alumni for support of colleges and universities, however, did not become commonplace until after World War I. As alumni contributions grew, so did the desire for alumni representation in institutional governing boards—a way to exercise continued donor influence. Cornell University was the first university to begin to place alumni donors on its governing board. At first, and differing from colonial donors from the local community, alumni donors favored mostly brick-and-mortar projects such as residence halls, libraries, student centers, or athletic centers. Alumni soon, however, began to establish endowed scholarships as well (Cutlip, 1965).

According to Cutlip (1965), systematic and organized fundraising is a phenomenon of the American twentieth century. Harvard ushered in the era of professional fundraising in 1919 when it hired the firm of John Price Jones to handle the institution's $15 million endowment campaign (Cutlip, 1965). Gradually, systematic fundraising moved from the elite colleges to institutions nationwide. The establishment of The Ohio State University Development Fund Association in 1940 initiated alumni fundraising campaigns in state-supported institutions (Meuth, 1992).

As state support for public higher education declined, more public two- and four-year colleges and universities began asking for gifts from individual donors in the latter half of the twentieth century (Thelin, 2004). Administrators began searching for all possible nontax revenue sources to help meet budget requirements. Supplemental public dollars "often [provided] the bulk of discretionary income for publicly supported institutions, and hence has been referred to as their margin of excellence" (Garvin, 1978, p. 7). Simply put, those universities that raise more funds have the ability to achieve more and surpass their competitors on many fronts, including rankings, student enrollment and retention, grants, and faculty recruitment.

As fundraising for both public and private colleges and universities grew in the later twentieth century, increased competition for dollars resulted. Nearly 2,000 private institutions and more than 1,500 public two- and four-year colleges and universities compete with each other for the same donations: "The competition for private dollars, both within the field of higher education and throughout the entire nonprofit world, is more vigorous now than ever before. For some institutions, doing well in this competition is no less than a matter of survival. For all institutions, competing successfully for private support provides the money to ensure institutional growth and strength" (Duronion and Loession, 1991, p. 1). In many ways, advancement offices' success or failure translates directly into whether administrations meet their educational and institutional goals.

According to Worth (2002), three main trends have marked the development of higher education fundraising since World War II. First, the field of fundraising became more professionalized. Colleges and universities began to hire internal fundraisers rather than using only the well-known fundraising firms such as John Price Jones and Marts and Lundy. As a consequence of the higher profile that fundraising attained, the chief development position rose to the most senior levels of college administration (Worth, 2002). Second, concerted efforts to raise voluntary support for institutions through the creation of well-organized development programs grew rapidly. Third, focus increased on large gifts, leading to a "narrowing of the fundraising pyramid," in which the largest gifts to higher education came from a smaller, wealthier segment of the population (p. 29).

Conclusion

Philanthropy from individual donors has defined and influenced American higher education since the founding of Harvard. The influence of donors on what is taught, how professional practice is executed, and even the allowance of women and blacks to receive an education have all been influenced by philanthropists. Simply stated, American higher education as we know it today would not exist if it were not for the voluntary contributions of many individuals.

More recently, as state support declined and institutional endowments fell in the economic downturn, the importance of philanthropy has perhaps become even greater to the survival of many institutions. In fact, Leslie and Ramey (1988) note that "voluntary support is becoming the only source of real discretionary money and in many cases is assuming a critical role in balancing institutional budgets" (pp. 115–116). As a result, it is important that institutions engage all possible donors. The approaches that most colleges and universities use are geared toward the population of alumni and donors that historically have had the disposable income to give philanthropically to higher education. With the growing middle- and upper-class of communities of color and an increasingly diverse alumni base, institutional advancement professionals must alter their practice. To engage alumni of color, they must recognize the cultural differences that affect philanthropic giving in communities of color.

Who Is Philanthropic?
Philanthropy by Nontraditional
Donors

> Philanthropy is commendable, but it must not cause the phil-
> anthropist to overlook the circumstances of economic injustice
> [that] make philanthropy necessary.
>
> — Martin Luther King Jr. [National Philanthropic Trust, n.d.]

PHILANTHROPY HAS LONG BEEN ASSOCIATED with "a relatively small number of white families and individuals [mostly men] who enjoyed access to education, owned major businesses, held leadership positions in government, dominated professions, and inherited wealth" (Council on Foundations, 1999, p. 7). This observation can be seen in the previous chapter through the past philanthropic influences on many institutions of today. But this definition of philanthropy or understanding of who is philanthropic is no longer acceptable. Research over the past twenty years has pushed to expand our understanding of who is philanthropic and to show how prosocial and philanthropic behaviors in communities of color and of women often differ—but still exist—from that of white men, who have traditionally been regarded as philanthropists. This chapter reviews the current literature on philanthropic giving in what has long been considered nontraditional donor communities.

Traditions of giving back, self-help, mutual assistance, and philanthropy exist in all racial and ethnic communities. Increasing numbers of people of color, long stereotyped as "charitable cases" rather than donors, donate their time and wealth to benefit their communities. Each community brings its own perspectives on giving, but much of the philanthropic world, including those raising funds and doing research on philanthropy, have overlooked the different methods and motivations for giving found among nonwhite wealthy communities. Institutions of higher education, and all nonprofits for that matter, benefit from understanding how different communities engage and participate in philanthropy. By understanding these differences, not only will individuals have deeper appreciation for their own philanthropy but institutions will also be more successful at engaging these populations that often are not motivated to give to higher education. Because communities of color are generous in fact, if institutions engaged in culturally sensitive fundraising, participation in gift campaigns by these communities would likely rise.

Overview of the Landscape

Gasman and Sedgwick's *Uplifting a People: Essays on African American Philanthropy and Education* (2005) focuses on the historical and contemporary ways that black communities have supported education through philanthropy by traditional and nontraditional means. Smith, Shue, Vest, and Villarreal's *Philanthropy in Communities of Color* (1999) looks at philanthropic traditions and behaviors in the black, Latino, Asian, and Native American communities. The authors convincingly show that philanthropy occurs in all communities regardless of race, ethnicity, and socioeconomic status. The book uses the authors' findings to suggest ways to secure contributions from these communities. Similarly, Pettey's *Cultivating Diversity in Fund Raising* (2002) provides strategies for fundraising in communities of color. And Capek and Mead's *Effective Philanthropy: Organizational Success Through Deep Diversity and Gender Equality* (2006) recommends strategies to strengthen racial and gender diversity in philanthropy.

In addition to these scholarly and practitioner-focused books, the Council on Foundations (1999) published *Cultures of Caring: Philanthropy in Diverse American Communities,* which examined potential ways to expand the use of institutional philanthropy. The report uses interviews of affluent donors from racial and ethnic minority communities as well as fundraisers, foundation staff and board members, tribal leaders, church clergy, and scholars to understand how these communities view philanthropy in their own cultural context. Using these books as a framework, this chapter explores giving in some of the nontraditional donor groups, including the African American, Latino, Asian American, and Native American communities. Because the most scholarship about philanthropy among communities of color is written about African American giving, it is the focus of this chapter.

African American Giving and Philanthropy

The majority of African American giving[4] and the organizations to which blacks give are centered on the ideas of racial uplift and the need to continue to overcome both historic and continued oppression (Carson, 1989b, 1993; Gasman, 2006b; Gasman and Sedgwick, 2005; Hall-Russell and Kasberg, 1997; Sweet, 1996). Hall-Russell and Kasberg (1997) described black philanthropy as "proactive rather than reactive. Rather than being an adaptive mechanism, it is a form of resistance to the exclusion African-Americans perceive from the majority community" (p. 13).

Fairfax (1995) suggests that black philanthropy is rooted in the African experience. She describes African American giving as a communal enterprise in which members are dedicated to and care for each other and contrasts this action with noblesse oblige charitable giving from the rich to the poor. According to Carson (1989b) and Gasman (2002), from slavery through the civil rights movement of the 1960s, African American philanthropy focused on giving among friends—gifts to churches, mutual aid societies, and fraternal organizations that provided funds locally and in their own communities. During the civil rights movement, black giving changed; African Americans began to give to "strangers" outside their immediate communities but still toward black causes and means of racial uplift (Carson, 1993). This type of giving benefited organizations such as the National Black United Fund and the United Negro College Fund (Davis, 1975).

Similarly, the Coalition for New Philanthropy in New York found that blacks born before passage of the Civil Rights Act of 1964 are more likely to support programs that focus their dollars on African Americans, while those born after the legislation are more apt to support nonprofits that benefit a larger spectrum of people (Gasman, 2006b; Mottino and Miller, 2005). Specifically, Mottino and Miller's study (2005) found that black donors from the pre–civil rights generation focus their current giving first on the church and then on educational institutions. This generation saw "the church not only as a religious and spiritual place but also as a center for community development" (p. 38). The top priority among younger generations is education. The church is often still a priority but to a lesser extent.

African Americans are not often thought of as philanthropic (Hodgkinson and Weitzman, 1988a, 1988b, 1990, 1992, 1994, 1996), but it is simply not the case. An Opinion Research Corporation (1990) survey of African American giving found that college-educated blacks and those that made more than $35,000 a year were more likely to be philanthropic than any other affluent, college-educated group. Additionally, a 2003 *Chronicle of Philanthropy* survey found that African Americans give a larger percentage of their disposable income to nonprofits than any other racial group, including the white majority (Anft and Lipman, 2003). This observation is confirmed by analysis of the Center on Philanthropy panel study that shows that differences in dollars donated is correlated with income, wealth, and educational level rather than race (Steinberg and Wilhelm, 2005).

Blacks are becoming wealthier. According to Havens and Schervish, (2005), who study wealth trends and have reported extensively on the pending wealth transfer (discussed earlier in this monograph), younger African Americans, those under forty-one years of age, have greater wealth than older African Americans. Further, Havens and Schervish (2005) calculated the wealth transfer in African American communities to be between $1.1 and $3.4 trillion dollars, with $40 billion to $283 billion going to charitable organizations (all figures in 2003 dollars).

As black Americans become wealthier, their giving will likely increase as well (Gasman, 2006b). Carson (1989a) argued that development officers should more actively appeal to the black community in an effort to engage them in the philanthropic process and encourage their generosity. Furthermore, according to Havens and Schervish (2005), it is important for organizations to "develop a longer-term strategy for the cohort of young wealthy African American professionals and business owners that may not at this time be affluent but will become very wealthy as their assets grow over the next two decades" (p. 55). Drezner's work (2008, 2009, 2010) on Millennial students at private historically black colleges and universities (HBCUs) begins to address Havens and Schervish's call for action.

Giving in the African American community remains, as it has in the past, focused on the church (Byrd, 1990; Carson, 1990; Community Foundation for Greater Atlanta, 2004; Gasman, 2002, 2006; Lincoln and Mamiya, 1990). In fact, Higginbotham (1993) believes that since slavery, the black church has been the "most powerful institution of racial self-help in the African American community" (p. 1). Gasman (2006b) found that donations to the church account for 45 to 90 percent of black philanthropy. According to the Center on Philanthropy and Civil Society (2004), African American support to social service organizations is the second-highest priority. Giving to organizations that directly serve the public need make up approximately 25 percent of black philanthropy. Health-related gifts, particularly to organizations that research and treat sickle cell anemia, diabetes, and HIV/AIDS make up 13 percent of philanthropic dollars (Community Foundation for Greater Atlanta, 2004; Gasman, 2006b).

African American Involvement in Educational Philanthropy

Education is recognized as a mechanism of racial uplift in the African American community (Elliott, 2006; Gasman, 2002, 2006b; Gasman and Anderson-Thompkins, 2003). Donations to education, including gifts to scholarships, institutions (including historically black colleges), or organizations such as the United Negro College Fund, account for 15 percent of black philanthropic giving (Center on Philanthropy and Civil Society, 2004; Gasman, 2007; Gasman and Anderson-Thompkins, 2003). Even so, African Americans are often not asked to donate, even to their own alma maters, and it is the most cited reason for African American communities' not participating in a fundraising campaign (Elliott, 2006; Gasman 2002; Gasman and Anderson-Thompkins, 2003; White House Council of Economic Advisers, 2000).

Black support of black colleges through the church. Although white industrial philanthropists have given large sums of money for the establishment and support of black colleges, blacks have supported their institutions from their founding as well, particularly through the black churches. Ellison and Sherkat

(1995) found that "throughout American history, the Black church has occupied a distinctive position in the individual and collective lives of African Americans" (p. 1415). One form of this "distinctive position" is the fundraising ability of the church through its members.

From Reconstruction throughout the civil rights movement and beyond, the black church is viewed as one of the most effective institutions at promoting the social needs of its congregants, according to Bishop John Hurst Adams. Research shows that African Americans often look to the church for advocacy, guidance, and the promotion of social needs in the community (Ellison and Sherkat, 1995). In turn, African American communities are committed to financially supporting the church to gain the community support that they seek from the religious institution (Gasman and others, 2011). Jones (1982) went so far as to say that "no institution or organization seeking to make an impact in Black communities could do so without the support of and cooperation of the churches" (p. 403).

Jones (1982) pointed to the historic connection between black church denominations and the development and support of black schools, pointing specifically to the power and agency of the clergy in the raising of money to establish and support black colleges and schools. "By 1900 Baptist bodies were supporting some 980 schools and 18 academies and colleges. The A.M.E. [African Methodist Episcopal] church raised over $1,000,000 for educational purposes between 1884 and 1900 and supported 22 institutions providing education above the elementary level. At the turn of the century, the A.M.E. Zion church was supporting 8 colleges and/or institutes, while the Colored Methodist Episcopal Church has established 5 schools during its 30-year history" (Jones, 1982, p. 404).

Beyond church support for black colleges, large collective and individual college movements have occurred to support black colleges outside a religious context. The next section discusses black agency in the philanthropic support of black colleges through the formation of the United Negro College Fund and other means.

Black college agency in fundraising. As mentioned, many scholars have explored individual philanthropists', particularly white industrialists', giving to black colleges, and others have looked at the black church's support of black colleges. Very few, however, have examined what individual black colleges did to raise funds on their own behalf. One example of such agency is creation of the United Negro College Fund.

The UNCF, established in 1944, is a comprehensive fundraising organization that solicits donations from individuals, corporations, and foundations. It provides operating funds for its thirty-nine members (private HBCUs) through scholarships and internships for students at hundreds of institutions and faculty and administrative professional training. Then-president of Tuskegee Institute Fredrick D. Patterson founded the UNCF after calling on his fellow private black college presidents to coordinate their own fundraising. Patterson believed that the private HBCUs would be more successful as a group than as individual institutions (Gasman, 2007). Gasman contended that "initially the UNCF seemed to be the perfect example of Black college agency: an organization started by blacks on behalf of black institutions. The real story is considerably more complex" (p. 3). Gasman portrayed an organization led by blacks but controlled by the white philanthropists who controlled the purse strings. Gasman (2001, 2003, 2007) found that for-profit fundraising firms such as Marts and Lundy were typically hired by white philanthropists to work with black colleges or at the suggestion of these donors rather than by the black colleges themselves. As a result of the black consciousness movement of the 1970s and the growing black middle class, black colleges began to emphasize hiring black fundraisers as a means to push back against the demands of white philanthropists and began truly leading the UNCF and the fundraising efforts of their own institutions (Gasman, 2007).

In an effort to understand black agency in the fundraising for black colleges, Gasman and Drezner (2008, 2009, 2010) looked at the work of the Oram Group, also a for-profit fundraising firm, hired by individual black colleges. These pieces investigated the partnerships that emerged between black administrators and white fundraisers in the 1970s. Gasman and Drezner (2009) found that "the combination of Black agency and the knowledge, access, and progressive views of the Oram Group [were] of utmost importance to the ultimate success of these campaigns" (p. 470). It was a new type of relationship between black colleges and those who help facilitate their fundraising—even in their relationship with the UNCF, which had a predominantly white fundraising staff until the 1970s (Gasman, 2007; Gasman and Drezner, 2009). Through the Oram group, black college fundraising moved from a "conservative and noncontroversial approach" to a progressive one that focused on social justice and the unique mission of black colleges (Gasman and Drezner, 2009, p. 470; see also Gasman, 2004). By looking at black agency in philanthropic support of black colleges, our understanding of philanthropy beyond wealthy white men begins to emerge.

Contemporary Alumni Giving to Historically Black Colleges and Universities

The Council for Aid to Education's annual Voluntary Support of Education survey reports that private liberal arts colleges rely on alumni support for 22.3 percent of their budgets (2004). In 2006, only fifty-two of the 103 HBCUs reported their alumni participation rates to either the Voluntary Support of Education or *U.S. News & World Report*. Of those reporting, alumni participation ranged from 1 percent (Grambling University, Prairie View A&M, and Texas College) to 38 percent (Claflin University in Orangeburg, South Carolina). These numbers are consistent with other findings. Gasman and Anderson-Thompkins (2003) found fifty-three historically or predominantly African American institutions reporting alumni participation in their study; of that number, half reported that 10 percent or fewer of the alumni donated funds.

Historically black colleges do not raise as much money as their predominantly white counterparts in either operational or endowment dollars (Gasman and Drezner, 2007; Yates 2001). Yates (2001) noted that in 1999, alumni participation at private liberal arts colleges was 32 percent, compared with 18.8 percent at public institutions. Alumni participation was 12.2 percent at black colleges in 2004 (Council for Aid to Education, 2004). This lower alumni participation rate might be the result in part of alumni misconceptions about the needs of their alma mater and the myth that black colleges are supported significantly by both the state and federal governments (Gasman and Anderson-Thompkins, 2003; Yates, 2001). Additionally, black colleges often rely on corporate and foundation giving to meet their voluntary contribution goals in their budgets (Drezner, 2005; Yates 2001). Yates (2001) suggested that corporate donors support black colleges to support their interest in hiring black college graduates to add to their corporate diversity. The corporate support of black colleges often makes alumni assume their participation in fundraising is not needed.

As noted previously, alumni gifts at HBCUs are considerably lower than alumni giving at predominantly white institutions. Gasman (2006a) noted that this finding could be attributed to the fact that African Americans hold fewer appreciated assets and earn less income than white Americans. "To be fair, many black colleges only recently began asking their alumni for contributions. And, many colleges don't call on their alumni to donate until 10 years after they graduate, thus missing the opportunity to establish a habit of giving on the part of recent graduates" (Gasman, 2006a, p. 1). As a result, it is considerably harder for black colleges to close budget gaps with alumni donations (Gasman, 2006a; *Journal of Blacks in Higher Education,* 1996).

All institutions of higher education, not just HBCUs, need to further engage black alumni (and all alumni for that matter). For example, by understanding African Americans' concern for and support of philanthropic causes that uplift the race, advancement professionals at colleges and universities can begin to engage their black alumni in ways that prospective donors can see their donations helping to further black students' education, going toward research that might cure diseases that disproportionately affect the black community, or making their campuses more welcoming for students of color.

Similar to philanthropy in the black communities, the cultural understanding and manifestations of Latino philanthropy differ from those of the white majority. The next section looks at giving among the multiple Latino populations.

Latino Philanthropy

Latinos, similar to African Americans, have historically been seen as nondonors (Hodgkinson and Weitzman, 1988a, 1988b, 1990, 1992, 1994, 1996). Ramos (1999) looked at the relatively low rate of "traditional" philanthropic participation among Latino Americans. A 1992 Independent Sector survey found that 53 percent of Latino households contributed to nonprofits, compared with 72 percent of all U.S. households (Hodgkinson and Weitzman, 1992). One explanation for this disparity is lower levels of disposable income among Latinos with respect to the larger American population (Ramos, 1999). Additionally, a large tradition exists in Latino communities of fictive kin networks and sending money to family members abroad. (Fictive kin are extended families often without formal blood or legal relations.) These forms of giving are traditionally not counted as philanthropy as they are not given through a nonprofit organization.

When philanthropy was defined more broadly than simply the giving of dollars to recognized nonprofits, including informal donations and to communities outside the United States, no statistical significance appeared in the difference of philanthropic nature in any racial or ethnic group (Smith, Shue, Vest, and Villarreal, 1999). Further, de la Garza and Lu (1999) found that when controlled for income, education, immigration, and trust in organizations, Mexican Americans gave and volunteered at the same rate as whites.

Additionally, Ramos (1999) pointed out, most Latinos come from nations where governments and churches rather than private and nonprofit organizations provide health care, education, and other essential services. As such, Latinos who recently immigrated to the United States or subsequent generations might not have a culture of support for education, as education is a true public good and fully funded by government and church. Given this context, it is not surprising that the vast majority of institutional giving among U.S. Latinos is to the church.

Smith, Shue, Vest, and Villarreal (1999) caution, in their look at Latino philanthropy, not to generalize and to believe that all Latino traditions of philanthropy are the same. They looked at giving and philanthropy in many of the different Latino subgroups, including Mexican Americans, Guatemalan Americans, and Salvadoran Americans and found that Mexican Americans often support large kinship networks beyond nuclear families, send large amounts of money to Mexico, and rarely volunteer in nonchurch, non-Mexican groups. Similarly, Guatemalan Americans often give of themselves through supporting their community by providing food and lodging to new immigrants. Much like Mexican Americans giving to kinship networks, Guatemalan Americans often give significantly to nonrelatives in their community. Interestingly, and of importance to higher education institutions, Guatemalan Americans in their study faulted U.S. organizations for being impersonal, greedy, and ignorant of Guatemalan traditions. Salvadorans, according to Smith, Shue, Vest, and Villarreal (1999), are more likely to give to well-established mainstream non-profits. Yet similar to Guatemalan Americans, Salvadorans distrust large charitable organizations.

Understanding how the different Latino subgroups often think about philanthropy can affect how universities should approach members of these communities for support. For example, by knowing that Salvadorans and Guatemalan Americans distrust large organizations, colleges and universities should take the time to inform potential donors in these communities about how their organizations work and how philanthropic support for the institution is used. By increasing the prospective donor's trust in the institution, they are more likely to give of their wealth.

Philanthropy to Hispanic Serving Institutions

Hispanic-serving institutions (HSIs) are a federally recognized group of institutions whose enrollment is at least 25 percent Latino. Mulnix, Bowden, and López (2002) looked at giving to these institutions. Noting that funding is a perpetual issue for HSIs and that federal funding is a political issue, Mulnix, Bowden, and López (2002) believe that HSIs must look toward private funding and support from alumni. They found that HSIs in general are very new to institutional advancement and that sophisticated, well-funded marketing, public relations, and enrollment management are necessary. Beyond this work, the literature contains a large gap as to how HSIs approach their alumni and others for philanthropic support.

Asian American Philanthropy

Similar to Latino philanthropy, Asian American giving generally focuses on supporting informal family networks that are not recognized as nonprofit organizations. Chao (1999) notes the trends among Asian Americans toward informal giving through care of extended family and community as well as giving to mutual aid societies, religious organizations, and Saturday schools. Chao found that Asian American giving is motivated by a strong ethic of duty and obligation, viewed as positive rather than negative. The concept of giving donations to endowments in return for tax deductions is a new concept for Asian Americans.

Japanese Americans are particularly interested in civil rights and civil liberties, although a generational component exists in Japanese Americans' support of these issues. Chao (1999) found that "second and third generation donors are more likely to give to social justice and civil rights causes and to have a stronger sense of philanthropy as a tool for civic and political participation" (p. 192).

Beyond civil rights support, education is the most frequently supported area by Asian Americans (Chao, 1999; Pettey, 2002). Chao (1999) found that, in general, Asian Americans prefer to support immediate needs rather than an endowment. Chao also found that Asian Americans place an importance on the accountability and effectiveness of the nonprofits they donate to, attributable to the fact that most wealthy Asian Americans are self-made. Endowment gifts, however, are often given to organizations that the donor or a family member personally benefited from. Pettey (2002) indicated that joint family gifts are appealing mechanisms for universities to engage Asian Americans.

Interestingly, Chao (1999) found that as Asian American donors become more familiar with other nonprofits, alma maters do not always remain the highest priority. It is therefore important that colleges and universities show the benefit of supporting one's alma mater as part of the cultivation process. Many interviewees in the Chao study spoke of isolation and loneliness in their college experiences, while others took pride in their being one of the first Asians to graduate from the school. Tsunoda (2010, 2011) reviewed the giving motives of wealthy Chinese Americans to American higher education and found many similarities between the giving of wealthy Chinese Americans and more traditional wealthy white philanthropists.

Again, like in other communities, understanding how Asian Americans think about philanthropy can be very beneficial to development officers. For example, knowing that many Asian Americans are more interested in supporting immediate needs than in supporting endowments might change the approach to soliciting Asian American alumni donations during an institution's comprehensive campaigns. Additionally, understanding the strong commitment to social justice among Japanese Americans might inform development officers about how to structure solicitations by placing the university's work in a larger social justice narrative.

American Indian Philanthropy

Like other communities of color but perhaps to a greater extent, American Indians are not considered philanthropic (Hodgkinson and Weitzman, 1988a, 1988b, 1990, 1992, 1994, 1996). Little has been written about American Indian philanthropy; a discussion of American Indian philanthropy is absent from the otherwise very strong work of Smith, Shue, Vest, and Villarreal (1999) and is only briefly introduced in Pettey's work (2002). Berry (1999), in her chapter on Native American philanthropy, notes that although many American Indian communities are still part of the poorest segments of American society, some nations have risen to new economic levels. She demonstrated that giving has always been a part of aboriginal community life and that philanthropy in the Native American nations rests on a system of mutual exchange, with each community member giving and receiving time, goods, knowledge, and blessings in addition to money. "For most Native communities, it is not new to share and exchange; it is new to institutionalize and standardize these activities" (Berry, 1999, p. 2). Even though support of people in one's community is not a new concept for American Indians, research on Native American philanthropy is seriously lacking and needs to be addressed. As American Indians increase their participation in higher education, having a better understanding of how to engage them in all aspects of the university, including alumni relations, is important.

Conclusion

Philanthropy among communities of color has many differences and nuances, but some themes—for example, the importance of family and kinship networks—emerge in a review of the literature. Most of the research reviewed here mentions how members of minority communities voluntarily give of their time and their wealth to support members of their nuclear and extended families, in their local community and abroad. Most of the philanthropy in these communities is given through nonmainstream, informal charities and organizations, often because of a distrust or lack of understanding of how nonprofits and universities work. One important result of informal giving is that much of these contributions go unreported on tax returns because they are not given to federally approved charitable organizations. Similarly, national surveys on philanthropic giving often do not count gifts from one person to another. This fact is very important to understanding why many communities of color that have strong traditions of giving have not historically been thought of as philanthropic: researchers have simply not been asking the correct questions and have been relying on tax regulations to guide their survey questions (see, for example, Hodgkinson and Weitzman, 1988a, 1988b, 1990, 1992, 1994, 1996).

Importantly, a 1992 Independent Sector survey found that blacks and Latinos are not asked to give at the same rate as the white majority. Further, Kaplan and Hayes (1993) reported that "these groups are even more likely to give when asked than other groups in the population" (p. 13). Higher education institutions should understand the giving traditions of their alumni and solicit them in culturally sensitive and appropriate ways.

Women and Philanthropy

Exploring the significance and variety of women's philanthropic action in education is important because both philanthropy and education were among the earliest spaces where women, though still acting within culturally prescribed roles, found opportunities to participate in the public sphere.

—Andrea Walton, 2005, p. 5

A S MENTIONED BEFORE, philanthropy has long been attributed to wealthy white men. This chapter briefly reviews the literature on women and philanthropy. Little scholarship exists that directly ties women and educational philanthropy, but one of the most significant contributions to the literature about women's historical involvement in educational philanthropy is Walton's *Women and Philanthropy in Education* (2005). In this volume, Walton and her colleagues show how prosocial behaviors—often in these cases gifts of time and the creation of local educational enterprises—should be viewed as as significant as large donations to our understanding of education today.

As mentioned, women have been part of higher education philanthropy since its beginning, first giving homemade candles, blankets, and other materials and eventually establishing women's colleges after their long exclusion from higher learning. Over the past few decades, however, women's visibility in philanthropy has greatly increased (Shaw-Hardy and Taylor, 2010). Given women's strengthened economic power (although it is important to note that income gaps still exist between the genders), women are just as likely to be philanthropists or to lead influential foundations and nonprofit organizations (Gasman and others, 2011). The philanthropic research on women's monetary giving to higher education continues to lag, however.

As with the discussion of philanthropy in communities of color in the previous chapter, understanding women's involvement in philanthropy has practical implications for universities. For example, women are playing a larger role in family economic decision making (Kamas, Preston, and Baum, 2008). Additionally, given the fact that women tend to live longer than men and because of the great wealth transfer discussed in the first chapter, significant philanthropic decisions will more likely be made by women.

Looking at philanthropy more generally can be very beneficial to our understanding of women's involvement and engagement in giving to higher education. Much like the historic thought that people of color are not charitable, women are often thought to be less generous than men (Capek, 2001). Again, this statement is incorrect. Capek (2001) notes that when accounting for variables such as age, income, number of dependents, and health, few differences are evident between men and women donors.

Complicating our understanding of women's philanthropic behavior is that findings conflict about how much and how often women give. In the literature on economics, research findings on generosity by gender are mixed (Bekkers and Wiepking, 2007; Cox and Deck, 2006). Some find that women are more generous and donate more than males (Andreoni, Brown, and Rischall, 2003; Bekkers, 2004; Carman, 2006; Croson and Buchan, 1999; Eckel and Grossman, 1998, 2001, 2003; Eckel, Grossman, and Johnston, 2005; Kamas, Preston, and Baum, 2008; Mesch, Rooney, Steinberg, and Denton, 2006), others find no difference (Bolton and Katok, 1995; Frey and Meier, 2004), and still others find men are more generous (Brown-Kruse and Hummels, 1993; Chang, 2005; Frey and Meier, 2004; Jackson and Latané 1981; Meier, 2007; Sokolowski 1996). Further complicating the literature, women are found to be more likely to give than men, but men give larger amounts (Andreoni, Brown, and Rischall, 2003; Bekkers, 2004; Belfield and Beney, 2000; Einolf, 2006; Lyons and Nivison-Smith, 2006; Mesch, Rooney, Steinberg, and Denton, 2006; Piper and Schnepf, 2008; Weyant, 1984). This phenomenon can be explained by the continued gender gap in income.

Some literature from sociology and social psychology suggests gender accounts for differences in motives for prosocial behavior, including monetary philanthropy and volunteerism. Scholars find that gender is a variable that affects giving, empathy, and altruistic behavior. Hoffman (1977) found that empathy is more prevalent in women than men and that women are more likely to experience guilt and a more highly developed interest in engaging in prosocial behaviors. Piliavin and Charng (1990) found that women are more charitable than men, but a meta-analysis on gender and helping behavior found that, despite inconsistencies among the studies reviewed, men help more than women (Eagly and Crowley, 1986). Others have found that gender difference was linked to religious and cultural commitments (Jha, Yadav, and Kuman, 1997).

Capek (2001) believes that "few sources of reliable data accurately document patterns of women's donating behavior or account for giving differences between women and men" (p. 2). For example, Hodgkinson and Weitzman (1996), reporting on the Independent Sector's biannual *Giving and Volunteering* study, found that married women give less than their spouses. But Boston College's Social Welfare Research Institute found the opposite, that women reported they gave more than men reported (Schervish, 1997). Further, among nonmarried individuals, giving patterns show little differences between the genders, although single women did report giving more often and at a higher percentage of their income than male respondents (Havens, 1994). Later Boston College research showed no difference (Schervish, 1997).

Volunteering

The majority of research shows that women volunteer significantly more than men (Einolf, 2006; Hodgkinson, Weitzman, Noga, and Gorski, 1992; Hodgkinson and Weitzman, 1996; Mesch, Rooney, Steinberg, and Denton, 2006; Sokolowski, 1996; Musick and Wilson, 2007). Some research studies show positive and significant relationships between monetary giving and volunteering (Brown and Lankford, 1992; Parsons, 2004). Furthermore, Parsons (2004) found female volunteers are more likely to give financially to the same organizations where they volunteer their time. Parsons concluded that volunteering helps women feel connected to the organization. This finding has important implications for universities and how they should engage alumni and other potential donors through volunteer opportunities.

Giving Decisions Among Couples

Among heterosexual married couples, Andreoni, Brown, and Rischall (2003) found that men tend to make most of the philanthropic giving decisions for a joint household. Education and income were more significant determinants than gender, however. Interestingly, they found that when women indicated that they are the primary decision maker about philanthropic giving, educational institutions such as their alma mater were more likely to receive a donation. Rooney, Brown, and Mesch (2007) looked specifically at gender and giving to education. Their findings were consistent with those of Andreoni, Brown, and Rischall (2003). Further, they found that when women made the decisions, the amount given to education increased as well. This finding also has significant implications for higher education and how development officers might engage heterosexual couples while cultivating and subsequently soliciting them. For example, it might be beneficial to involve an alumnus's wife in the cultivation of a potential gift, even if she is an alumna of another institution.

Organizational Choice

Women, much like in communities of color, tend to donate their time or wealth to organizations that have affected them or someone close to them (Burgoyne, Young, and Walker, 2005; Parsons, 2004). Andreoni, Brown, and Rischall (2003) found that men concentrate their giving among a small number of nonprofit organizations, while women are more likely to spread their philanthropic giving across a larger number of organizations. Further, Einolf (2006) and Rooney, Brown, and Mesch (2007) found that women are more likely to give to education institutions and organizations than men. Others found no statistical difference between men and women when it comes to alumni giving (Okunade, Wunnava, and Walsh, 1994; Wunnava and Lauze,

2001). Okunade (1996) found that men donate significantly more than women when looking at dollars given. Wunnava and Lauze (2001) found that women were more regular donors, while men, though giving less regularly, gave more significantly to higher education. Looking specifically at alumni giving to a large public research university over fifteen years, Okunade, Wunnava, and Walsh (1994) found no statistical difference in men's and women's giving.

Conclusion

The literature concerning women's philanthropic giving is far from clear. Many studies conflict about how women give, how much, and how often. What is clear, however, is that women are philanthropic, and, as their economic power grows, their ability to engage in significant philanthropy does as well. By understanding the research—even though often conflicting—colleges and universities might think about how they engage alumnae and the strategies that they might use to solicit them.

What Guides the Study of Philanthropy and Fundraising?

> Every dollar makes a difference. And that's true whether it's Warren Buffett's remarkable $31 billion pledge to the Gates Foundation, or my late father's $25 check to the NAACP.
>
> —Michael Bloomberg [National Philanthropic Trust, n.d.]

COLLEGE AND UNIVERSITY ADVANCEMENT OFFICES ponder why donors give freely and how to encourage alumni to make regular financial contributions to their alma mater. What motivates alumni and other donors to make financial contributions to their alma mater? This chapter explores the answer to that question as presented in the literature to ground the study of philanthropy and philanthropic behavior in theory.

This chapter presents the theoretical frameworks that guide most of the research on philanthropy and fundraising. These theories come from a number of disciplines and paradigms. Scholars from the disciplines of economics, psychology, and sociology have all contributed to our understanding. This chapter looks at the different perspectives of the public- and private-good models and the psychological and sociological paradigms. It is important to note that many of the theories that currently exist were created using research that almost exclusively looked at the giving of wealthy white men. Therefore, much of the literature reviewed in this chapter does not take into account the diverse cultural approaches that are brought to view and the ways in which philanthropy is enacted in racial and ethnic groups and often among women.

Motivations

People give of themselves and their wealth by engaging in volunteerism and philanthropy for many reasons. Although debate continues about whether "true altruism" exists, most scholars agree that many philanthropic gifts and prosocial behaviors are motivated by a blend of altruism and self-interested motives. The level at which donors think of themselves and their self-serving interests obviously varies. Some gifts might be given out of a motivation to receive recognition, which is an extreme form of egoism. An example might be a person who gives a large sum of money to have an endowed chair, college, or building named on his or her behalf to be recognized.

A more nuanced motive for giving is the idea of mutual benefit. Mutual benefit, in the context of philanthropy and volunteerism, is the donor's or volunteer's receiving some level of intrinsic or extrinsic gain from the action to assist others. Donors whose giving is considered highly altruistic and recipient oriented—for example the anonymous donor who in 2009 gave $70 million to twelve institutions led by female presidents with the caveat that there must be total anonymity, not just to the public but also to the institution and anybody associated with it—likely still derive some personal benefit from their gift. This personal benefit might be a sense of self-worth or as Andreoni (1989) called it, a "warm glow." Other forms of benefit for donors include recognition by the organization for their gift in myriad ways, including a listing in the annual report, naming of an endowed scholarship, entrance to an exclusive event, a small thank you gift, or the tax deduction given for contributions.

In the context of volunteerism, Clary and Snyder (1990) found that, like for philanthropic giving, volunteers are motivated by a combination of altruism and personal benefit. Volunteers seek personal growth through wanting to join a group of colleagues or aspirational peers professionally and in social networks, to learn or enhance a skill, or even to assuage guilt. Again, the level of egoistic motives compared with altruistic intentions varies in each individual and with regard to the situation as well.

The Public Good Versus Pure Altruism

One of the most common reasons that people engage in prosocial behavior, volunteerism, and philanthropy is out of a want to help others—the concept of altruism. Roberts (1984) defined altruism, through an economic lens, as "the case where the level of consumption of one individual enters the utility function of the other" (p. 137). In other words, donors or volunteers disregard their own self-interest to help others. The idea of selflessness has been studied widely in many academic disciplines, including economics, sociology, and social psychology (Bergstrom, Blume, and Varian, 1986; Piliavin and Charng, 1990; Ribar and Wihelm, 2002; Roberts, 1984; Sugden, 1982; Warr, 1982, 1983; Wilson, 1975).

Many economists argue that philanthropic giving lies within the public good model. In economics, the public good model assumes that a need, or good, that is consumed by one individual does not reduce availability of the good for others. In other words, a public good does not lie in a zero-sum game. In the context of philanthropy, economists argue that a donor gives of himself or herself out of an altruistic concern to maximize the public good among others. The concept of the public good and pure altruism from an economic sense, however, allows only for giving to offset a direct need rather than to supplement a need. In other words, an increase in one person's (or the government's) contribution results in a decrease of other people's (or the government's) contributions (Sugden, 1982; Vesterlund, 2004). The economic concept of crowding out, in its simplest form, explains that the reduction of private investment in a public good occurs because of an increase in government spending on that good. Using this concept, Roberts (1984) and Warr (1982) found that theoretically government contributions to nongovernment organizations and other nonprofits supporting public goods would "crowd out" private contributions dollar for dollar. Levy contends that philanthropy might actually crowd out the government's responsibility to its citizens (see "Who Gives?").

The Private Good

Philanthropic giving and other forms of prosocial behaviors do not only help the recipients. The donor and volunteers often benefit as well. In the coming sections I explore some of the ways in which people benefit intrinsically from giving of themselves.

Identification model. Many studies of the motivations of donors have found that an aspect of a donor's "self" is present in the decision to engage in philanthropic behavior (Jackson, Bachmeier, Wood, and Craft 1995; Martin, 1994; Schervish, 1993, 1997, 2003; Schervish and Havens, 1997). Schervish and Havens (1997) found that many donors see themselves in "the needs and aspirations of others" (p. 236). Jackson, Bachmeier, Wood, and Craft (1995) found many voluntary gifts are made out of "the sense of being connected with another or categorizing another as a member of one's own group" (p. 74), which they refer to as "we-ness." When donors identify with a cause, their identification might trigger their motivation to make a contribution. In higher education, it can be as simple as a former scholarship recipient's deciding to give a scholarship to a student at their alma mater, recognizing that they might not be as successful as they are had not someone done the same for them. According to Martin (1994), mutual benefit comes from prosocial behavior, as "philanthropy unites individuals in caring relationships that enrich giver and receiver alike" (p. 1).

Becker's rational utilitarianism theory (1974, 1976) is the basis of the identification model. Becker pushed back on the idea that pure altruism exists, arguing that many who give of themselves have a desire to improve society. Donors are also motivated by a form of peer pressure, or extrinsic motivation, however, "to avoid the scorn of others or to receive social acclaim" (1974, p. 1083). Schervish and Havens (1997) reflected on Becker saying that the "selfless" in altruism is actually "grounded in a form of mutual self-interest" or, as Becker described it, "multiperson altruism" (1976, p. 237).

Schervish and Havens (1997) argued that the identification model encompasses five theoretical interrelated clusters: models and experiences, communities of participation, frameworks of consciousness, direct requests, and discretionary resources. A donor's experiences lead to his or her personal moral ideology, which affects participation in an organization based on belief in the group's mission; solicitations for support of these nonprofits occur in these communities of participation. Finally, the amount that a donor gives is subjective and connected to his or her disposable income. Analyzing the 1992 National Survey of Giving and Volunteering through the lens of identification theory, Schervish and Havens found giving behaviors were more closely related to the donor's current communities of participation than to his or her prior experiences. Additionally, Jackson, Bachmeier, Wood, and Craft's study (1995) found that religious participation increased philanthropic behaviors toward secular organizations. It was most typical among those who defined themselves as actively involved in the church (p. 74). This finding is not surprising, as charity and philanthropy are the cornerstones of all religions (Gasman and others, 2011).

Martin (1994) defined community as "any group of people joined by shared caring, both reciprocal caring in which they care about the well-being of members of the group and of caring for the same activities, goals, or ideals" (p. 26). In his definition of community is the idea of reciprocal caring relationships—the idea that donors might have some reciprocal benefit even when giving anonymously or giving to someone they might not know. Sugden (1984) refers to this phenomenon as reciprocity theory. In the context of higher education, this concept of a reciprocal benefit is often espoused. One example is solicitation for the annual fund. Often universities remind alumni, especially young alumni, that part of the *U.S. News & World Report* rankings is tied to alumni participation in giving and that by giving even a small amount to the alma mater, a graduate might help increase the university's ranking and thereby the value of the degree.

With Martin's thoughts on community in mind, many economists have considered the motivation for giving beyond the position of the public goods theorists who emphasize altruism. These economists argue that some donors give for private good benefits (Andreoni, 1989, 1990, 1998; Cornes and Sandler, 1984; Palfrey and Prisbrey, 1996, 1997; Steinberg, 1987; Sugden, 1984). In economic terms, Andreoni's "warm glow" is an additional personal benefit that a donor receives from engaging in prosocial behavior.

Andreoni (1988, 1989, 1990) referred to this phenomenon as "impure altruism." Andreoni's studies disagree with the findings of Roberts (1984) and Warr (1982). Andreoni found that the government's crowding-out effect is incomplete and that those who give to the public good do so for two reasons—to increase the public good and to receive some aspect of private good from the gift (Andreoni, 1998).

Impact philanthropy. Building on the motivations of public and private good for philanthropic behavior, Duncan (2004) suggested that some donors hold an extreme desire to "make a difference" (p. 2159). Calling these donors "impact philanthropists," Duncan suggested that contributions by these individuals are motivated to increase the output of a charitable good. The concern about the impact philanthropy model is the potential dependence between donor and recipient. Recently, academic centers have begun to study how wealthy donors might best "invest" their philanthropy to get the highest return on investment. The Center for High Impact Philanthropy at the University of Pennsylvania uses academic research in the fields of business and social welfare to provide information and tools for donors (Noonan and Rosqueta, 2008). Others have called this type of philanthropy "venture philanthropy" (Boverini, 2006). This recent philanthropic movement is associated with donors' providing not only the means but also the expertise, typically in the area of organizational capacity building (Boverini, 2006).

Social Psychological Perspectives

Social psychology or the study of the relations between people and/or groups is a natural interdisciplinary academic home for the examination of philanthropic and prosocial behaviors. Social psychology also allows for the study of how situational factors affect the thoughts, feelings, and/or behavior of individuals. In the following sections I explore many of the different social psychological perspectives.

Relationship marketing and social exchange theory. Relationship marketing and social exchange theory are often seen as the conceptual foundation of fundraising. The relationship fundraising model in development is derived from marketing theory (Burnett, 1992/2002; Kelly, 1998). Relationship marketing, defined as "establishing, developing, and maintaining successful relational exchanges" (Hunt and Morgan, 1994, p. 20), is one of the most prevalent. In other words, relationship marketing is the idea of establishing long-term relationships with alumni to maintain their loyalty, involvement, and donations (Gamble, Stone, and Woodcock, 1999; Kotler, 1997; McKenna, 1991). Relationship marketing is predicated on the benefit of customer retention and a customer's lifetime value to a company (Buttle, 1996; Sargeant and McKenzie, 1998). This idea is easily combined with continuity theory, which states that repeated actions are more likely to be continued and sustained (Atchley, 1989), suggesting that those who have established giving relationships are likely to give repeatedly (Lindahl and Winship, 1992; Okunade and Justice, 1991; Piliavin and Charng, 1990).

Building relationships between the institution and its current and prospective donors is arguably the most important aspect of successful solicitation of the largest or (leadership) gifts. In the past, fundraising offices relied on transaction-based marketing. In other words, each year donors were asked to give, and a series of one-time transactions took place. Relationship marketing changes fundraising strategy from a series of one-time transactions to a focus on the donor's lifetime giving (Sargeant and McKenzie, 1998).

Another popular reason that people give is social exchange theory. Similar to the concept of mutual benefit, it is based on the belief that "voluntary actions of individuals that are motivated by the returns they are expected to bring and typically do in fact bring from others" acquires social recognition (Blau, 1992, p. 91). Many scholars apply social exchange theory to philanthropic and volunteer motivations (Cook and Lasher, 1996; Hollander, 1990; Simon and Ernst, 1996). Hollander (1990) and Simon and Ernst (1996) looked at the effect of social approval on voluntary actions. Simon and Ernst (1996) found, through a controlled experiment, that among strangers, social exchange theory is not effective in increasing voluntary cooperation. Among groups of people that know each other, however, the influence of wanting to be accepted and noted for their actions has an effect.

According to Kelly (1991), "Fundraising predominantly involves a social exchange relationship between a charitable organization and a donor, in which the power of each relative to the other determines the outcome of the exchange" (p. 199). Cook and Lasher (1996) built on Kelly's work (1991) in the context of higher education. Their study advanced the idea of how different university players, including presidents, trustees, volunteers, deans, and advancement professionals, engage donors in different ways to connect the university and donors' needs.

More specifically, Cook and Lasher (1996) and Kelly (2002) used social exchange theory to explain the interdependent relationship that exists between donor and alma mater. Under this model, alumni donate when they understand that their interests align with the needs and interests of the institution. Kelly (2002) found that "based on social-exchange theory, the mixed motive model of giving describes two levels of donor motivation: (1) raising the amount of common good . . . and (2) receiving some private good in return" (p. 46). These mixed motives, evident in social exchange theory, align with the intrinsic and extrinsic influences of prosocial behavior (Harbaugh, 1998).

Social identity theory and organizational identification. Organizational identification, a part of social identity theory, occurs when an individual defines himself or herself by an organization. In the context of higher education, "I am a student at . . . " or "I am an alumna of . . . " is a good example of organizational identification (Ashforth and Mael, 1989; Mael and Ashforth, 1992). Mael and Ashforth (1992) suggest that college alumni conceptualize organizational identification perfectly: "(1) College can be considered a 'holographic organization' (Albert and Whetten, 1985), that is, one where members share common organization-wide identity and are less likely to experience competing demands from, say, department-level or occupational identities, and (2) since alumni constitute a particularly critical source of support for colleges, alumni identification is likely to strongly affect the welfare of their respective alma maters" (p. 104).

Mael and Ashforth (1992) proposed correlates of organizational identification in which aspects of both the institution and the individual feed into an alumnus's organizational identity, which then leads to an "organizational consequence" of his or her supporting the alma mater (Figure 1). Using social identity theory as a basis, Mael and Ashforth (1992) predicted that alumni identification with their alma mater corresponds to participation in gift campaigns, alumni relations events, and encouragement of others to attend the institution. They found that organizational characteristics such as how distinctive and prestigious the institution is believed to be have positive effects on organizational identity. Further, Mael and Ashforth believed competition between similar schools increases alumni identity. Institutional tradition and prestige were also found as factors that influence alumni contributions (Leslie and Ramey, 1988).

Competition in an institution for alumni identity and participation has a negative effect, however. In other words, if multiple departments or offices

FIGURE 1
Proposed Correlates of Organizational Identification

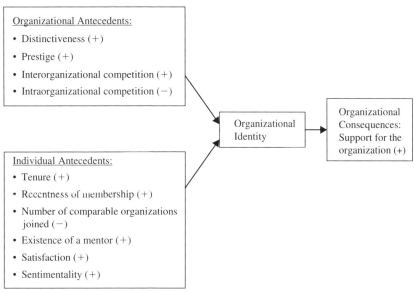

Source: Revised from Mael and Ashforth, 1992, p. 107.

compete for alumni support without an organized effort, alumni participation falls (Mael and Ashforth, 1992). Additionally, Mael and Ashforth (1992) identified individual characteristics that affect a person's organizational identity. They found that time spent at the institution, the existence of a mentor, overall satisfaction, and perception of the graduate's time at the college or university (sentimentality) all have positive effects. Additionally, recentness of participation positively affects organizational identity, while those with more than one alma mater often have a weaker organizational identity with each institution then those who attended only one university.

Mael and Ashforth's model (1992) predicts that having a positive institutional identification leads alumni to make a donation to their alma mater but not all alumni with positive feelings about their college or university choose to support the institution financially or through service after graduation. It is important to note that Mael and Ashforth (1992) do not explain how certain alumni with positive organizational identities decide to support their alma mater over those who do not.

Minority-serving institutions perhaps have a better opportunity to create the personal and organizational identity that Mael and Ashforth (1992) suggest. Gasman and Anderson-Thompkins (2003) found that "for many Black-college alumni, the bond to alma mater is formed long before they arrive on campus—especially in the case of legacies. . . . The college is 'alma mater' in the truest sense because it nurtured them much like a mother and gave them skills that they might not get elsewhere in a White-dominated society. If nurtured and re-kindled regularly, the surrogate parent image can be beneficial to institutional fund raising; if neglected, it can be devastating to alumni giving" (pp. 37–38). Drezner (2008, 2009, 2010) found that it is this "bond to alma mater" and the UNCF that the National Pre-Alumni Council and private HBCUs develop and enhance through stimulating the interest and participation of students enrolled at member institutions.

Other researchers have agreed with and expanded Mael and Ashforth's findings. For example, Miller and Casebeer (1990) found that increased student involvement in institutional activities positively affected alumni giving. Gaier's research (2005) also supported this observation: "Alumni who participated in at least one formal student activity during the undergraduate experience were 87 percent more likely to give" than those who were not engaged as students (p. 285). Others have found that involvement in alumni activities increased giving to their alma mater (Bruggink and Siddiqui, 1995; Hunter, Enid, and Boger, 1999; Mosser, 1993; Taylor and Martin, 1993; Young and Fischer, 1996). Moreover, Leslie and Ramey (1988) found that the economic success of alumni factored into their ability and desire to support their college. Further research found that emotional attachment between the graduate and his or her institution was a factor influencing contributions (Brittingham and Pezzullo, 1989; Mosser, 1993; Spaeth and Greeley, 1970). And alumni and alumnae academic success and overall happiness with their student experience increased the likelihood of alumni gifts (Gaier, 2005; Miller and Casebeer, 1990).

Alumni success is not the only predictor of increased alumni giving. Harrison (1995) predicted the probability of alumni giving based on the amount of money spent on fundraising and alumni relations. Using statistical modeling, Harrison showed that the old adage that "you have to spend money to make money" is true for alumni fundraising. He found that an increase in spending for alumni relations of as little as $10 per current student could increase alumni participation from 25 percent to 26.4 percent, which could significantly increase dollars raised.

Model of personal donorship. Related to social exchange theory is Mount's model (1996) of personal donorship, which posits that donors decide the level of their giving based on five criteria: (1) involvement in the organization, (2) the importance of the mission with respect to the donor's other philanthropic obligations, (3) self-interest, (4) the donor's disposable income, and (5) past giving behavior. Mount's research showed that tax incentives have only a nominal impact on giving.

Justice motivation theory. The pervasive need to fix an injustice might be a motivation to engage in philanthropic giving and volunteerism. Lerner (1975) and Miller (1977) refer to this need to believe in a just world as a "justice motive." Warren and Walker (1991) applied this concept to philanthropic giving, finding through mail solicitations in Australia that "if people witness undeserved suffering their 'belief in a just world' is threatened; consequently they are motivated to restore their faith. . . . This motivation may lead to helping behavior, but only if the person believes [his or her] actions will be of real and permanent help" (p. 328). In the context of higher education, one can easily imagine an annual fund letter or phone call asking for alumni support for scholarships. Warren and Walker's findings suggest that the solicitation for these scholarships must have more than a compelling case for support—such as helping a returning student whose parents were recently laid off. Rather, the solicitation should show how the gift will have a lasting impact on both the students receiving the scholarship and on the institution's ability to continue to serve other students who might need financial help to remain on campus.

Prosocial behavior. Another notable theory that examined donors' motivation from a psychological perspective is the prosocial behavior approach

(Clark, 1992; Dawes, Van de Kragt and Orbell, 1990; Diamond and Kashyap, 1997; Hogg, 1987; Midlarsky, 1971; Piliavin, Dovidio, Gaertner and Clark, 1981; Schwartz and Ben-David, 1976). Eisenberg and Mussen (1989) defined prosocial behavior as "voluntary actions that are intended to help or benefit another individual or group of individuals" (p. 3) and explored prosocial behavior from the vantage point of the recipient rather than that of the one taking the action—in other words, such behavior is the consequence of the action, not necessarily the motivation to act in a helping manner. Prosocial behaviors can include volunteering, giving money, comforting, rescuing, or helping others. The activity of prosocial behavior should not be confused with altruism, which is a motivation to help others regardless of the benefits to the one doing the action. For example: An alumna gives a multimillion-dollar gift to the university to establish need-based scholarships. She asks that her name not be associated with the gift and that she not even be recorded in the alumni database as a donor or given a tax receipt in recognition of her gift. The alumna's gift might be motivated by a level of altruism, as she is not receiving any recognition or economic gain, but the actual donation is the prosocial action.

The concept of prosocial behavior was first introduced in the 1970s by biologist Edward Wilson (1975), who found evidence that humans and other animals would help one another in different ways. His findings led to the development of the field of sociobiology. Building on Wilson's findings, social scientists (more specifically, developmental psychologists) contend that prosocial behavior is a biological function rather than solely nurtured or learned actions. Social psychologists have shown, however, that prosocial behaviors, while a natural function, can also be taught and learned (Eisenburg, 1982; Rushton, 1982; Schroeder, Penner, Dovidio, and Piliavin, 1995).

Prosocial behavior with its psychological foundation is an important conceptual framework for the understanding of philanthropic actions. Philanthropy is one form of prosocial behavior. Philanthropy can be defined by its Greek origin, the "love of mankind," as voluntary action for the good of others. Bentley and Nissan (1996) suggest that prosocial behavior explains the circumstances in which people act to help others and how the inclination to give of one's self exists.

According to social psychologists, it is possible to learn prosocial behavior (Eisenburg, 1982; Rushton, 1982; Schroeder, Penner, Dovidio, and Piliavin, 1995). Therefore, the act of giving alumni donations to one's alma mater can be learned. Studies show that as a person ages, developmental and moral reasoning can evolve in terms of helping others. The following chapter discusses teaching youth and students philanthropic behavior.

Philanthropic modeling. Bentley and Nissan (1996) explored how primary school students learn philanthropy and altruistic behavior. The study suggests that witnessing an influential adult (parent or guardian, teacher, religious or youth organization leader) engage in acts of philanthropy is most effective in passing along the importance of helping others. Schervish and Havens (1997), using the 1992 Survey of Giving and Volunteering in the United States, found that witnessing at least one parent or guardian engage in volunteer work, watching a family member help others, or being the recipient of help while young was associated with higher levels of giving as an adult.[5] Hunt (1990) referred to it as "modeling theory." This teachable moment is intensified when it is coupled with a discussion about the importance of such actions (Bar-Tal, 1976; Bentley and Nissan, 1996).

One example of parental modeling is found in Rosenhan's research (1970). He studied deeply committed and involved civil rights volunteers and found that their sense of action and volunteerism was born out of their home environment. Additionally, Cascione (2003) found family influences and experiences affect the motivations of major gift donors in higher education: "Participation drew directly from their family backgrounds and was assisted by the historical milieu in which they were living. Having individuals who are able to teach generosity through their actions and lifestyles plays a crucial role [in] carrying on a philanthropic tradition. Role modeling represents a form of teaching philanthropic values and individuals who represent such generosity encourage others by their actions. Extraordinary acts of generosity become ordinary events and since they are seen as ordinary events, the ability to replicate them would be a typical response in the course of an individual's life" (p. 69).

Finally, the most effective tool is for the child to participate in giving and volunteerism to help reinforce the positive feelings associated with helping others (Bentley and Nissan, 1996). Hodgkinson and Weitzman (1996) found that among those who have seen a family member help another person or family member, 73.6 percent make charitable contributions; while of those who do not recall seeing a family member give, the probability of donating is only 50 percent. Parental actions also affect children's in-kind philanthropy such as volunteering. Bekkers (2003) correlated adult children's volunteering with recollections of their parents' volunteering. Other scholars have found that adults influence children in teaching values such as philanthropy as well (Bremner, 1996; Grusec and Kuczynski, 1997; Steinberg and Wilhelm, 2003a).

Researchers have found that providing opportunities for community service helps children learn not only the positive feelings associated with prosocial actions but also the importance of philanthropy (Daloz, 1998; Schervish and Havens, 1997). In her review of the current literature, Bjorhovde (2002b) therefore concluded that "the acquisition of the value of philanthropy and its resulting behaviors of giving and serving are the consequences of three primary types of learning: (1) modeling, which involves seeing and hearing, (2) cognitive learning, which combines thinking and discussing, and (3) experiential learning, which involves doing" (pp. 9–10). Having looked at many of the theoretical frameworks and theories that can guide one's research on philanthropic behavior, we will now look at some of the theoretical frameworks more specifically in the context of higher education.

Applying the theories to higher education research. Historically, development officers did not rely on theory to guide their practice. Even today, most fundraising literature is written for practitioners offering supposedly "best" practices that are often not grounded in theory (Brittingham and Pezzullo, 1989; Carbone, 1986; Kelly, 1991). According to Broce (1986), "Fund raising as a professional process is best understood broad[ly] . . . . [It] encompasses the entire operation from goal identification to gift solicitation" (p. 27). By further understanding donors' motivations and successful fundraising strategies from a theoretical standpoint, future research on philanthropy and fundraising will allow practitioners to enhance their advancement programs, expanding them to new prospect pools by better understanding how donors choose to participate in a prosocial manner.

Donor motivation includes the prior willingness to give and the factors that influence the action. Motivation is the foundation of giving. A successful gift is received when the donor's motivation is combined with proper cultivation and solicitation (Paton, 1986). Pezzullo and Brittingham (1993) suggested that a variety of donor characteristics influence giving, including the desire to affect the public good, "the desire to buy acclaim and friendship, the need to assuage feelings of guilt, the wish to repay society for advantages received, egotism, . . . investment in activities that have indirect utility to the donor . . . or tangible perquisites" (p. 31). Pickett (1986) concluded that donor motivation includes belief in the organization, obligation, community needs, ego positioning, self-interest, and self-actualization. When looking specifically at college and university alumni constituencies, Connolly and Blanchette (1986) suggested that donors' motivation declines steadily as alumni age because they identify with their college or university less than more recent graduates would. This finding agrees with Mael and Ashforth's (1992) organizational identity theory described above. Therefore, engaging young alumni and students with opportunities to remain connected to their alma mater is extremely important (Nayman, Gianneschi, and Mandel, 1993; Van Nostrand, 1999). Additionally, according to continuity theory (Atchley, 1989), once an alumnus or alumna makes a first gift, even as a student, the likelihood of future donations is enhanced.

Development officers have long known that alumni who attend a university on scholarship are often motivated to return this generosity by contributing to—or creating—scholarships at their alma maters. Cascione's research of major donors (2003) found that those who were scholarship recipients viewed the awards "as a form of institutional investment in individuals" and recognized that some payback was in order (p. 99). Cascione's research also recognized that receiving a scholarship is often a college student's "first practical experience of the effects of . . . philanthropy" (p. 99).

Having a high-quality relationship with a mentor while in college often motivates donors to give to their alma mater (Cascione, 2003). Most of the literature devoted to academic mentors is written about graduate students rather than undergraduates (Lovitts, 2001; Nettles and Millett, 2006). Cascione found, however, that some donors gave to their undergraduate institutions in appreciation of a faculty mentor.

A graduate's kinship with his or her alma mater is often an important motivator in giving. As mentioned previously, Mael and Ashforth (1992) correlated organizational identification with contributing. Development officers often use this connection between alumni and their alma mater—school spirit—when soliciting donations, whether through impersonal telemarketing and direct mail or the very personal individual request for support.

Gasman and Anderson-Thompkins (2003) investigated the motivations of alma mater among black college alumni, noting black college alumni's "sentiments of honor, devotion, and duty" (p. 36). Black alumni in their study repeatedly used language such as "nurturing" and "culturally uplifting" to describe their college experiences (p. 36). Further, according to their study, advancement officers at black colleges recognized this "incredible bond" and worked to harness these emotions, directing them into alumni involvement as volunteers and donors (Gasman and Anderson-Thompkins, 2003).

The use of intrinsic and extrinsic motivations for participation. Colleges and universities regularly solicit their alumni for donations, using intrinsic and extrinsic benefits as motivation. Extrinsic motivators may include small gifts, invitations to campus or alumni activities, a listing in widely read annual reports, membership in giving societies, or the belief that alumni participation and dollars increase their alma mater's reputation and therefore the value of their own degrees. In contrast, intrinsic motivations include giving to a scholarship to help others attend college (Harbaugh, 1998).

Sansone and Harackiewicz (2000) debated the value of extrinsic and intrinsic motivations. Social learning theory suggests that students' involvement in a group that encourages forms of philanthropy (monetary, service, for example) influences students' socialization and organizational identity, ultimately increasing their prosocial behaviors (Rushton, 1982). Friedmann (2003) suggested that as a result of this socialization process, intrinsic motivations of prosocial behavior would have a greater influence than extrinsic motivations. Students in organizations that encourage philanthropy such as student-alumni associations could more easily understand the needs of institutions and therefore participate in annual campaigns at a higher rate (Friedmann, 2003). Kang (2005), in a study of Korean individual giving and volunteering, found that experience in contributing during school years significantly and positively affects future giving patterns. Therefore, student philanthropy programs to support the institution or other charitable causes might be beneficial to future alumni fundraising (Drezner, 2010).

Schervish (1993) asserted that a person's philanthropic identity is established by means of motivating factors such as involvement in a "community of participation." He suggested that participation in an "organizational setting in which philanthropy is expected or at least invited by the fact of being active in the organization" (p. 33) strengthens the donor's identity with the community by virtue of the socialization process.

Giving by young alumni and students affects future donations. By engaging young alumni in the college or university "community" of donors, institutions will potentially benefit for years to come. Building on Atchley's continuity theory (1989), Lindahl and Winship (1992) and Okunade and Justice (1991) found that past giving behaviors are positively correlated with current and future giving practices. Continuity theory suggests that colleges can establish relationships that will continue long after graduation. Cascione (2003) referred to this phenomenon as "reinforcement theory" in the context of higher education. Giving by young alumni, even in small amounts, can establish a pattern of contributions that will persist for a lifetime (Lindahl and Winship, 1992; Monks, 2003; Nayman, Gianneschi, and Mandel, 1993; Okunade and Justice, 1991). The next chapter discusses in more detail how to engage students and young alumni in fundraising.

Conclusion

The theoretical frameworks needed to understand philanthropy and to guide the practice of fundraising come from the disciplines of economics, psychology, and sociology. Each theory provides a conceptual home for the study of philanthropy and how it can affect higher education and how colleges and universities might engage their donors. As mentioned earlier, the study of philanthropy has occurred for only the past thirty years, and its study in the context of higher education has been for an even shorter time. Because the vast majority of the literature concerning philanthropy and fundraising for higher education is atheoretical, stronger research and practice should be developed using theories to support that work.

Using these theories demands caution, however, as they were developed using a mostly white wealthy male view of how philanthropy is defined. Continued research is needed on how to expand and develop new, more inclusive theories of philanthropic motivations and behaviors.

Engaging Students and Young Alumni: The Importance of Cultivating the Next Generation of Donors

> So the education in giving goes on from generation to generation. It is not merely the gift that counts or the help that is given the neediest; it is the acquainting of the families year after year, as children grow into youth and youth into manhood and womanhood, with the conditions about them and the cultivation of the habit of giving.
>
> —"Generation to Generation," *The New York Times,*
> December 17, 1937

COLLEGE AND UNIVERSITY MISSIONS often espouse ideals such as creating an active and engaged citizenry. One manifestation of citizenship is prosocial behavior, or voluntary actions toward others. Philanthropy is one example of prosocial behavior. It, coupled with the growing need for voluntary dollars to support operating budgets and the subsequent need to engage as many alumni as possible in giving to an institution, brings to the forefront a question of how college and universities might engage students and young alumni in general to be prosocial and more specifically to support their alma mater upon graduation and beyond. This chapter reviews the current literature on how young people, including school-aged children, college students, and young alumni learn to be philanthropic—generous with their time, talents, and wealth.

Studies show that as a person ages, developmental and moral reasoning can evolve in terms of helping others (Drezner, 2010). Young children offer help as a result of extrinsic motivation: being told to help, wishing to avoid punishment, being promised a gift or prize. Less tangible benefits such as peer approval are associated with adolescent motivation to help others. Adults reach a different stage, in which intrinsic feelings motivate their prosocial behavior (Bar-Tal, 1982; Cialdini and Kenrick, 1976; Eisenburg, 1982; Kohlberg, 1985; Schroeder, Penner, Dovidio, and Piliavin, 1995). When children perform prosocial acts and receive positive feedback, they internalize the praise and think of themselves as "good" (Miley, 1980; Rosenhan, 1978). As they repeat these actions and grow older, children experience increased levels of moral obligation, and their need for external motivations is reduced (Piliavin and Charng, 1990). Schroeder, Penner, Dovidio, and Piliavin (1995), reviewing other research, suggested that prosocial behavior can be taught and learned. Many believe that direct reinforcement as well as observing and discussing altruism influence prosocial behavior (Ahammer and Marray, 1979; Grusec, 1982, 1991; Israel, 1978; Moore and Eisenberg, 1984; Rushton, 1975, 1982; Smith, Gelfand, Hartmann, and Partlow, 1979).

Undergraduate students' involvement in alumni and fundraising activities at institutions is a community of participation that creates a strong foundation for active alumni support after graduation. In a 1981 interview about his involvement in founding the United Negro College Fund in 1944, James P. Brawley, then president of Clark College (now Clark-Atlanta), understood the importance of instilling a culture of giving in undergraduates so that they are more likely to donate as alumni:

> If you are going to develop responsive alumni you don't do it by talking to them when they are in their caps and gowns ready to go, and then expect them to respond by giving handsome gifts to the college. . . . The need is to develop a systematic plan for the alumni to contribute and stimulate their interest through what is done while they are at the college for four years, and if you don't get a good response out of them during those four years, the chances are 99 [percent] that you won't get much of a response after they have gone [Brawley, 1981].

Substantial literature agrees with Brawley's principle and discusses the importance of engaging students in fundraising (for example, as solicitation callers) and even as donors early in their careers at both two- and four-year institutions (Chewning, 1993; Kerns, 1986; Lynch, 1980; Nakada, 1993; Nayman, Gianneschi, and Mandel, 1993; Purpura, 1980; Shanley, 1985; van Nostrand, 1999).

Nayman, Gianneschi, and Mandel (1993) suggested that "turning students into donors is a socialization process that involves orienting students to the notion of voluntary giving, actively engaging them in varied institutional advancement activities, and strategically timing program initiatives" (p. 90). By socializing the students in this way, the authors found that students are more likely to participate in future fundraising campaigns. As mentioned before, according to Atchley's continuity theory (1989), established patterns are likely to be followed in the future. Further research shows that giving from young alumni, even in small amounts, has potentially large effects on lifetime donating (Lindahl and Winship, 1992; Monks, 2003; Nayman, Gianneschi, and Mandel, 1993; Okunade and Justice, 1991; Piliavin and Charng, 1990). The impact of engaging young alumni in giving to their alma mater can be significant. In fact, some research from other private research universities shows that the vast majority of $1 million–plus donors begin to give in their first ten years out of school (Monks, 2003). Meer (2008) found that alumni who gave to their alma mater annually in the five years after graduation gave, on average, eight times more to their institution by their twentieth reunion than even those alumni who donated the same amount in the first few years but did not develop a steady habit. The gifts that Monks (2003) and Meer (2008) looked at were given by alumni long after their graduation. The next section looks at how giving differs by generation.

Giving Across the Generations

Steinberg and Wilhelm (2003b), using the Council on Philanthropy Panel Study, found statistically significant data that the prewar generation (born before 1945) is more generous than Generation X (born between 1965 and 1981), even after adjusting results to remove the impact of wealth and other differences. Using constant dollars, the prewar generation annually gives $1,764 per person, baby boomers (born between 1945 and 1964) $1,254, and Generation X

$1,100. In other words, Generation X is about one-third less generous than the prewar generation. Little is known about Millennials' giving (those born between 1982 and 2001), which could be simply because of their young age and life situation. Millennials, however, are known for their volunteering. According to a survey on volunteering, teenagers in this generation volunteer on average of 125 hours per year, nearly double the figure found ten years earlier (Oates, 2004). It is important to note that in the same time period, more and more high schools required community service to graduate.

Given Steinberg and Wilhelm's findings (2003b) that the younger generations give significantly less than their parents and former generations, Steinberg, Wilhelm, Rooney, and Brown's findings (2002) that inherited money is less likely to be donated than earned money, and the Bush administration's repeal of the estate tax, nonprofits have cause for concern. To counteract this trend, an understanding of how a culture of giving is instilled is necessary. The next section looks at the current literature that examines how youth learn and are often encouraged to be prosocial.

Engaging Youth in Philanthropy

Youths' engagement in philanthropy is the focus of many nonprofit organizations and foundations. Between 1988 and 2003, the W. K. Kellogg Foundation gave more than $100 million in grants "to help fund the promotion and development of youth engagement in social, civic, and community building" through volunteerism, service, and philanthropy (Ho, 2003, p. 2).

Teaching Philanthropy

Bjorhovde (2002a, 2002b) identified four concepts that she believes should be part of any formal or informal philanthropy curriculum: factual, motivational, procedural, and personal development. The factual concept introduces the learner to giving as the "critical societal force" in American culture through teaching about philanthropy's history, relationship with government, and role in the community (2002b, p. 13). The reasons that people are philanthropic and the idea that anyone, regardless of personal wealth, can be a philanthropist through in-kind gifts of time and service are part of Bjorhovde's motivational concept. The procedural and personal development concepts include teaching ways for students to get involved and how their actions help others (Bjorhovde, 2002a, 2002b).

Combining Bjorhovde's types of philanthropic learning and curricular concepts provides an interesting model to use in the ivory tower. Drezner (2008, 2009, 2010) found that by engaging students with opportunities to learn about and participate in community service, civic engagement, service-learning projects, and student alumni associations such as the National Pre-Alumni Council (NPAC) at private HBCUs, the institution cultivates a generation of engaged alumni dedicated to future service to the university. Astin and Sax (1998) and Astin, Sax, and Avalos (2008) also discuss how participation in service during college affects students' philanthropic behavior.

The NPAC, according to Drezner (2008, 2009, 2010), socializes and cultivates new groups of donors from the Millennials by motivating students with gifts and opportunities that are appropriate for the developmental stage of college students. Further, the use of messages and opportunities to participate in racial and community uplift adds to the NPAC's success and participants' desires to be involved. The NPAC's educating students about the importance of giving and needs of the institutions has been vital in students' decisions to be involved as donors and fundraisers.

Although not all institutions have a mission to be sources of racial uplift for their students, alumni, and communities as minority-serving institutions such as HBCUs and tribal colleges and universities do (Gasman, Beaz, and Turner, 2008), all institutions can learn from the successes of the NPAC in the socialization of students as future donors and active citizens. The next section reviews the limited work that looks at how student affairs and advancement officers can work together in this work.

Student Affairs and Advancement

There is limited literature on interactions between advancement offices and student affairs divisions. There have been two edited volumes focused on fundraising in student affairs; they are both part of the *New Directions for Student Services* series published by Jossey-Bass (Volume 63, 1993; Volume 13, 2010). Additionally, there have been some works published by NASPA;

however, little work has been published focusing on philanthropy and fundraising. This section reviews the scant literature on this topic.

Student affairs divisions' involvement in fundraising has grown over time, yet at many universities such a division is still nonexistent. A 1993 study found that the majority of student affairs programs were not asked to assist in soliciting funds and did not see fundraising as part of their job responsibilities (Terrell, Gold, and Renick, 1993), but the authors reported that the overwhelming majority of student affairs campus leaders acknowledged that they should be involved in fundraising. Beyond the lack of student affairs practitioners involved in fundraising, Fygetakis and Dalton (1993) noted that more than 8.5 percent of institutions responding to their survey did not have an advancement officer assigned to student affairs. According to a 1997 survey conducted by the National Association of Student Personnel Administrators (NASPA), this amount increased to 30 percent (Penney and Rose, 2001). It is important to note that these development officers are only very rarely responsible for student affairs divisions and have other campus fundraising responsibilities.

The NASPA weighed in on the topic in a 2001 book, *Dollars for Dreams: Student Affairs Staff as Fundraisers* (Penney and Rose, 2001). *Dollars for Dreams* is a practitioner-oriented book that educates student affairs administrators about the principles of fundraising. Student affairs fundraising is most typically targeted to parents and specific alumni groups (Penney and Rose, 2001). Student affairs officers and advancement officers continue to increase their campus partnerships (Miller, 2010). Understanding the importance of students' experiences for alumni satisfaction and future giving, Rissmeyer (2010) noted that "the daily work of student affairs lays the foundation for successful fundraising" (p. 22).

With the review of the theoretical underpinnings of the study of philanthropy and fundraising completed, the next chapter turns to a review of the studies looking at who donates to higher education and other nonprofits.

Who Gives?

> The most useful and influential people in [America] are those who take the deepest interest in institutions that exist for the purpose of making the world better.
>
> —Booker T. Washington [National Philanthropic Trust, n.d.]

WHAT INCREASES THE PROPENSITY to support higher education, and how might we use this knowledge to be better fundraisers? This chapter discusses what the emerging research says about education's effect on philanthropic giving. The conclusion of the chapter includes suggestions about how colleges and universities might combine this knowledge with alumni data already in their databases.

Numerous empirical studies show that a positive relationship exists between a person's level of education and the propensity to engage in prosocial behavior, in particular to donate money (Apinunmahakul and Devlin, 2004; Banks and Tanner, 1999; Bekkers, 2003, 2006; Bekkers and De Graaf, 2006; Bielefeld, Rooney, and Steinberg, 2005; Brooks, 2004; Brown, 2005; Brown and Ferris, 2007; Brown and Lankford, 1992; Carroll, McCarthy, and Newman, 2006; Chang, 2005; Chua and Wong, 1999; Duncan, 1999; Eschholz and Van Slyke, 2002; Feldman, 2007; Gruber, 2004; Houston, 2006; Jones and Posnett, 1991; Kingma, 1989; Lyons and Nivison-Smith, 2006; Lyons and Passey, 2005; Matsunaga, 2006; McClelland and Kokoski, 1994; Mesch, Rooney, Steinberg, and Denton, 2006; Olson and Caddell, 1994; Pharoah and Tanner, 1997; Reece and Zieschang, 1985; Reed and Selbee, 2002; Rooney, Steinberg, and Schervish, 2001; Schiff, 1990; Schlegelmilch, Diamantopoulos, and Love, 1997; Sokolowski, 1996; Tiehen, 2001; Todd and Lawson, 1999; Van Slyke and Brooks, 2005; Wiepking and Maas, 2006; Wilhelm, Brown, Rooney, and Steinberg, 2006; Yamauchi and Yokoyama, 2005; Yavas, Riecken, and Parameswaran, 1981). Furthermore, Schervish and Havens (1997) found that as a person's level of education increases, the likelihood of his or her charitable giving being a larger proportion of income rises as well. In a previous study, however, Feldstein and Clotfelter (1976) found no difference in giving between college graduates and those with less education once they controlled for wealth, income, and tax bracket.

Results are mixed as to whether or not a person's level of education affects his or her charitable contributions to religious organizations, churches, synagogues, and mosques. Hoge and Yang (1994) found a positive relationship between education and religious giving for Protestants but did not find the same relationship for Catholics. Yen (2002) found that no relationship exists between education level and religious giving but found that as one's education rises, a positive relationship exists with the support of secular nonprofits.

Level of education does not affect the likelihood of a person's giving to nonprofits with a mission to help the poor or human service organizations (Regnerus, Smith, and Sikkink, 1998; Marx, 2000). Further, a 2002 study of donors to the American Lung Association found that level of education was negatively correlated with giving to health-related nonprofits (Keyt, Yavas, and Riecken, 2002).

Some scholars look at the relationship between specific degrees and majors and the propensity to give and at what level. For example, Wunnava and Lauze (2001) found that social science majors were most generous to their alma maters at small liberal arts colleges. Similarly, Hillygus's work (2005) shows that social science majors were more likely to volunteer after controlling for a number of variables such as income level. Bekkers and De Graaf (2006) similarly found that those with social work and other social science degrees tend to be more generous.

Business school and economics graduates were more likely to donate to their alma mater than other alumni (Blumenfeld and Sartain, 1974). Because this study did not control for income, however, the increased likelihood of donating might be a result of having a better income than other graduates.

Similarly, Okunade, Wunnava, and Walsh (1994) found greater generosity among business and economics graduates, but they too lacked income measures. Bekkers and De Graaf (2006) found no difference in economics majors' charitable donations when comparing them with other alumni.

Marr, Mullin, and Siegfried (2005), looking exclusively at Vanderbilt University, found that economics, mathematics, and social science majors were more likely to donate to their alma mater. When controlling for income, they found that performing arts and science majors were less likely to do so. Also when controlling for income, Monks (2003) found that young alumni graduates from private universities with an MBA or law degree gave larger amounts to their alma mater than those without a professional degree. Further, Monks found that fine arts and nursing majors gave significantly less, while history degree recipients gave significantly more than other humanities majors. He did not find any other differences among other majors.

Briechle (2003) found that alumnae specifically at sectarian schools were motivated by three factors: (1) knowing of the university's mission; (2) loyalty for the institution; and (3) believing that their gift would make a positive impact. He found that the women in his study were loyal to their alma mater overall as well as to their department and other aspects of the college experience, demonstrating the importance of the ability to segment solicitations. Additionally, with regard to the positive impact of the gifts, the women's responses indicate the importance of universities' being able to clearly show how gifts are being used and the difference that they make.

Briechle (2003), when looking at alumnae of public and private (nonsectarian) schools, found that a feeling of obligation was an important reason that they chose to give. This obligation was often linked to wanting to pay forward any financial assistance the women received as students. This finding aligns well with Dugan, Mullin, and Siegfried's results (2000) that young alumni at Vanderbilt were 12 percent more likely to give if they received need-based grants. Interestingly, Dugan, Mullin, and Siegfried also found that the probability of a young alumnus or alumna's making a gift to Vanderbilt dropped 13 percent if they received need-based loans. This difference might be because the young graduates felt that their loan payments were a way that they were still "giving" to the institution (Monks, 2003).

Monks (2003) also looked at recent alumni giving and found that a number of campus experiences were associated with future alumni giving. Those young alumni who lived on campus and participated in cocurricular activities such as student government, intercollegiate athletics, performing arts, fraternity and sorority life, or campus religious life were more likely to give. Those students who were active in a campus political organization were less likely to give, however.

Monks (2003) also looked at young alumni's academic experiences and their effect on future giving. He found that alumni who had internships, contact with faculty outside of class, and significant relationships with their advisors or campus staff were more likely to donate to their alma mater, while those who had less interaction, for example, those engaged in independent study or research or individualized majors, were less likely to give.

With an understanding of how college attendance and experiences affect an alumnus's or alumna's likelihood of giving, we now look at how institutions might use data that they might already have to create stronger, more strategic fundraising programs.

Adding Science to the Art of Fundraising: The Power of Using Data in Fundraising Strategy[6]

To have a strong fundraising program, it is important for universities and colleges to have a strong prospect research program. Prospect researchers are tasked with identifying donors who are likely to give significant gifts to the university based on capacity and interest. Beyond prospect research, it is important for fundraising programs to have strategies that are dynamic and respond to the specific aspects of different segments of alumni pools. By understanding donors, prospects, and nondonors through the information and data collected, more informed decisions about fundraising strategy can be made.

Why Use Data?

Not too long ago, development offices consisted of calling cards and many paper files. With access to less expensive, smaller, and more powerful computers, the management of prospects has drastically changed. Large data sets are now commonplace, and segmentation in the annual fund and other mass mailings that were once nearly impossible is now rather simple. Birkholz (2008) suggested that "like the emergence of volunteer-driven fundraising and the creation of voluntary associations, data mining is the next great breakthrough in the fundraising industry. Its impact on development programs will be as great as any change in the past 50 years" (p. xiv).

It is common knowledge that the most successful fundraising strategies all involve personal solicitations that take into account prospective donors' interests. It is simply impossible and cost prohibitive, however, to personally ask each prospect. Using the data collected about prospects and donors can help to understand these individuals, thereby making annual fund and other mass mailing solicitations more personal. The use of data can add a personal solicitation aspect to traditionally less personal fundraising tactics.

It is not to say, however, that the multiple relationships donors have established with organizations and development officers are no longer important. Rather, using analytical data can bolster those relationships. As Birkholz (2008) rightfully noted, "The new tools of analytics, when combined with centuries of insights about private giving support and volunteering, open new possibilities to build upon the current practices of fundraising and to further the important work of philanthropy" (p. xv). Data collected from personal contacts and prior mailings, phone calls, and event responses can tell a great deal about how to develop future strategies and segmentations.

What Can an Institution Tell from the Data?

The information that can be gained from data is limited only by the data collected. By looking at data such as date of gift, solicitation code (how the institution asked for the gift), and payment method, simple data mining can help identify donors' giving patterns and behaviors that can lead to their retention and even upgrades of the amount they give. For example, an advancement office can explore when their donors typically give. Do they respond to end-of-fiscal-year calls for action? Do they prefer to give at the end of the tax year? Do they respond to "crisis" solicitations? What is their solicitation preference? Direct mail? E-solicitations? Telephone calls? How do they give? Online? Check? Credit card? With this knowledge, an advancement office can segment mass solicitations by time of year and solicitation method that will be more successful and cost-effective.

More complicated analysis of donors' behavior and knowledge of past solicitations—who gave and who were solicited without success—can reflect donors' priorities for giving to the organization. For example, which donors are more likely to give to a special project such as library acquisitions or emergency scholarship aid, and who responds well to requests for purely unrestricted dollars? As the organization tries new messages to communicate a case for support, understanding the data can help determine not only how effective that message might be but also with whom it was most effective and the groups for which strategies should change.

An Example of Data Mining

Wylie and Sammis (2008), who have both written and worked extensively on data mining for the nonprofit world and more specifically for higher education, have developed some simple models to show the power of data. One report looked at a model employed over time at five different higher education institutions. Using their model and donor data each university provided them, they created a score for each alumnus or alumna that predicted the likelihood of their giving to their alma mater. After making their predictions, they monitored the same graduates' giving to see whether their predications were correct. They found the scores predicted with good accuracy alumni giving over multiple time intervals (some models were tested within an interval of a few months, others with multiple years). Wylie and Sammis found that if the institutions had used the scores that the predictive models produced to segment their annual fund appeals, the institutions would have known where to focus their efforts, saving money and resulting in much higher participation rates.

A Cautionary Note

The power of data is extreme, and it can also send development officers down wrong paths. To reach the goals of efficiency (minimizing fundraising costs) and effectiveness (maximizing growth in giving), some might interpret the data so that they might not want to continue to solicit and engage a certain segment of their database. Before making such a decision, fundraisers have an obligation to take a step back and see whether there is something more than what the data suggest. For example, if data mining in a college suggests that a large segment of alumni of color should no longer be solicited as they have not given before, the institution's administrators should ask themselves how they are not serving this population and what they could do differently. A growing body of literature looks at philanthropic giving in communities of color and how it differs in motivation and practice from the white majority (see, for example, Smith, Shue, Vest, and Villarreal, 1999; Pettey, 2002; Gasman and Anderson-Thompkins, 2003). Understanding these differences and the fact that the first principle of fundraising is that people give because they are asked, the strategies employed must be reviewed before these people are written off and opportunities explored to engage these populations in a more culturally sensitive way.

Using data in the creation and implementation of fundraising strategies is the centerpiece of the Fundraising Effectiveness Project, a joint initiative of the Association of Fundraising Professionals and the Center on Nonprofits and Philanthropy at the Urban Institute. The Fundraising Effectiveness Project looks to help nonprofits increase both efficiency and effectiveness. By understanding the power of data, collecting it, and analyzing it, all nonprofits can reach both of these coveted ideals while also raising the dollars needed to fulfill their respective missions. The use of data in fundraising allows strategy to be "grounded in facts, not assumptions" (Birkholz, 2008, p. 3).

Allowing data to help guide strategy will never make traditional development officers and their personal understanding and experiences obsolete. In fact, development officers' knowledge of donors' motivation and practice will always be needed to fully interpret the analytics that will come from statisticians. Birkholz (2008) reminds us that "it is easier for fundraisers to be successful when they are armed with the knowledge of context and implementation than it is for statisticians armed only with technology. When knowledge and technology come together, the potential is limitless" (p. 210). In the end, using data does not take the "art" of advancement away; it just adds the science.

A Critical Look at Philanthropic Giving

> The idea of charity unites dominant class interests and human values into one seamless web. Charity promises its clients salvation through normalization; it promises normalization through friendship. Charity promises its contributors social tranquility through community; it promises salvation through the simple act of sending money. The idea of charity forms its multiple moralities: Charity becomes a sacred morality of religion, an all but sacred morality of democratic community, an economic morality of capitalism, a human morality of compassion for others.
>
> —Donileen Loseke, 1997, p. 440

THE POWER OF PHILANTHROPY is great and rarely disputed. It can open doors for opportunity, save lives, and allow lives to be enriched. Like everything, however, it has the potential for harm, and it is necessary to critique the actions, motives, and outcomes of individual, foundation, and corporate philanthropy. Since 1912 *The New York Times* has appealed to its readers to give to its "Neediest Cases Campaign"; in 1937 one contributor pointed out that giving "make[s] life richer, more beautiful and lovely for both giver and receiver" (cited in Loseke, 1997, p. 440). How do an individual's, foundation's, or corporation's motives and the larger societal context affect the meaning and outcome of philanthropic donations?

Philanthropy toward American higher education cannot be removed from the context of our capitalist economy. Gordon (1975) noted, it is the tension between "the political principles of democracy and the economic principles of capitalism," involving a call for equal rights yet unequal incomes (p. vii). Labaree (1997) addressed this tension in the context of education by pointing to the different purposes of education: to create active and engaged citizens (democratic equality); to train workers and professionals (social efficiency); and to allow for social mobility. This chapter looks at some of the most common critiques of philanthropy and places it in a higher education context.[7]

One of the main critiques of philanthropy is that it contradicts the capitalist free market (van Fleet, 2010). One example of this contradiction is corporate philanthropy (Brown, 2004). van Fleet (2010) notes that neoliberal economists suggest the free market "resolves inequalities through its automatic invisible hand adjustments." Liberal neoclassical economists contend that the free market does not allocate resources efficiently. As a result, government might intervene to support what is deemed to be a public good such as education. The inherent contradiction exists in between an altruistic type of philanthropy that has no motive and the capitalist free market that has a continual motive of maximum profits.

Philanthropic giving is at its basic level a reallocation of resources, often from an individual, corporation, or foundation to a population with less wealth than the donor or donors. In the free market system, a neoliberal economist views philanthropy as an intervention or disruption in the allocation of resources in the free market (van Fleet, 2010). Liberal economists view philanthropy as a needed reallocation of resources to correct inequities but view this reallocation as the duty of the government (Levy, 2006; van Fleet, 2010).

The nonprofit or third sector in which the actions of philanthropy lie has a unique relationship and interaction with both government and the private sector of society. Many scholars have looked at philanthropy's placement in the larger society (see, for example, Mertens, 1998; Paton, 1991; Schuppert, 1991; Smith, 1991; Van Til, 1988). Each of these models has the third sector interacting with the state and the market in some way, and an inherent tension exists among the actions of the three different sectors. The role of philanthropy is often at the center of this tension. Andrew Carnegie, in his famous essay "Wealth," asserts social welfare should be the prerogative of the rich as trustees for the poor, while Senator David Walsh critiqued philanthropic activities as an attempt to remove government's responsibility and ability to provide public goods.

A number of scholars have deemed philanthropy a means for providing essential services to citizens as morally problematic (Alperovitz, 2005; Edwards, 2008; Giroux, 1998; Levy, 2006; Shiva, 2003). Levy (2006) argued that "donations directed at providing essential services to our fellow citizens [are] morally problematic" and noted that "all essential services ought to be provided to our fellow citizens by government, not by philanthropic organizations" (p. 163). In essence, Levy argued that leaving public goods to philanthropy renounces government's obligation to its citizens. In other words, in our context, higher education should be viewed as a public good, and resources should come from the government rather than from individual, foundation, or corporate philanthropy.

Levy and others therefore have argued that education should be provided for by the government through taxes.[8] These critics believe that when a government provides a service such as education, the community is able to hold them accountable. If citizens are unhappy, they can protest and call for change through elections, but it is not the case when foundations and wealthy individuals make the decisions through philanthropy.

Another concern about philanthropy is that personal self-interest cannot be removed from our understanding of philanthropic motivations. Numerous scholars have examined how foundations use their philanthropy to push their missions and their opinions (Arnove, 1980a, 1980b; Karoff, 2004). Berman (1980a, 1980b, 1982) examined foundations' effect on education in developing countries and their work outside the United States after World War II. He found that "foundation overseas programs and development strategies . . . were frequently coordinated by intermediate organizations established or funded by one of the foundations. . . . These programs and strategies were neither exclusively humanitarian in purpose nor apolitical—foundation disclaimers notwithstanding" (Berman, 1982, p. 48). Similar criticisms can be made about individual motives for giving, in particular about large gifts from venture philanthropists who give gifts with many benchmarks and requirements of the university receiving the gift.

Income inequality exists in capitalism, and another critique of philanthropy is that it can perpetuate this social inequality. Philanthropic scholars of education, particularly industrial philanthropists, have debated whether this outcome is purposeful or might have been accidental (Anderson, 1988; Anderson and Moss,

1999; Curti and Nash, 1965; Jencks and Riesman, 1967; Lewis, 1994; Sowell, 1972; Watkins, 2001). Giroux (1998) warned that this concern about exploitation, creation, and perpetuation of inequalities has been a historical concern about corporate power. "History has been clear about the dangers of unbridled corporate power . . . Four hundred years of slavery, ongoing through unofficial segregation; the sanctioning of cruel working conditions in coal mines and sweatshops; and the destruction of the environment have all been fueled by the law of maximizing profits and minimizing costs" (p. 15).

The greatest set of critiques of foundation giving is found in Arnove's *Philanthropy and Cultural Imperialism: The Foundations at Home and Abroad* (1980b). Many of the contributions in this monograph explore philanthropy's connection with the reproduction of class structures in society. Arnove and his colleagues found that "foundations like Carnegie, Rockefeller, and Ford have a corrosive influence on a democratic society; they represent relatively unregulated and unaccountable concentrations of power and wealth [that] buy talent, promote cause, and in effect, establish an agenda of what merits society's attention" (1980b, p. 1). He believes that foundations can be responsible for the "production of culture and the formation of public policy" through their giving practices (p. 1).

Booker T. Washington (1910/2008) suggested that providing resources to educate marginalized people, blacks in his case, was one way to "accomplish the greatest good in this generation" (p. 25). Many historical and contemporary examples exist, however, where philanthropic giving results in the opposite effect—perpetuating or increasing inequality. Arnove (1980b) further contended that philanthropy can lead to cultural imperialism in which the "ethnocentrism of an elite group from a particular class and cultural background . . . [arrogates] the right to determine public policies in critical areas of culture not only for U.S. society but other societies as well" (p. 2).

The Supreme Court ruling in *Brown* v. *Board of Education* not only called for the desegregation of elementary and secondary public schools but also shaped black colleges and their relationships with foundations for decades (Gasman and Drezner, 2009). Gasman (2007) found that within the context of the struggle for racial integration finding financial support for "all-black" institutions became increasingly difficult. Gasman found that some foundation leaders assumed that black colleges would not be around in the coming years. Foundation dollars to black colleges dropped significantly during the first few years after *Brown*. Giving to black colleges did not return in significant levels until the early 1970s (Gasman, 2007; Gasman and Drezner, 2008, 2009, 2010; Trent, 1981). In fact, during the civil rights era, foundation leaders decided to support a few black colleges such as Atlanta University, Dillard University, and Fisk University (the Ford Foundation from 1955 to 1980). Administrators of the Ford Foundation believed that the "elite" black colleges were strong enough to potentially recruit white students and therefore would likely integrate (Mays, 1987, p. 38; Gasman, 2007). Rather than acknowledge the strengths of black colleges for the students who attended them, foundation leaders believed they knew what was best for higher education and black students. Foundation leaders thought that it was best to support the colleges and universities with the greatest capacity and those deemed the strongest by the foundations (Kimball, 1981).

Of course, individual industrial philanthropists had used this approach since the early years of black colleges (Anderson, 1988). One of the ways the Carnegie and Rockefeller Foundations perpetuated social inequality through the funding of education initiatives occurred in the early 1920s. Both Carnegie and Rockefeller funded the work of Edward Thorndike. His foundation-sponsored "research" was used to support initiatives to change the courses of study for black students from the liberal arts to "realistic and industrial" subjects (Thorndike, 1929; Marks, 1980). He justified these different educational approaches because in his mind "each individual by sex, race, hereditary equipment and the circumstances of time and place in which he is born, is made likely to meet certain situations rather than others during life, and it is to be competent and happy in those situations that he particularly needs to be taught. It would be wasteful to train the Jews and the Negros identically" (Thorndike, 1912, p. 23). Segregated education in the South was a by-product of this philanthropic giving by foundations (Spring, 2004). The concept of industrial education received the further support of the industrial philanthropists who benefited from vocational education's production of inexpensive labor (Anderson, 1988; Lewis, 1994; Spring, 2004; Watkins, 2001). Andrew Carnegie philanthropically supported industrial education of blacks because "he believed that educating black workers was necessary to maintain the United States' position in the world economy . . . [stressing] the importance of maintaining proper work habits among the black southern population" (Spring, 2004, p. 53).

As mentioned earlier, scholars have paid significant attention to white industrial philanthropists and their support of black colleges between 1865 and 1930. Jencks and Riesman (1967) along with Curti and Nash (1965) and Sowell (1972) viewed the industrialists' support of black colleges and education initiatives as altruistic—both "generous and benign" (Gasman and Drezner, 2009, p. 2). More recently, however, revisionist scholars began to view these efforts as self-serving in an effort to control the South's labor market and create an enduring underclass of black workers (Anderson, 1988; Lewis, 1994; Watkins, 2001). More contemporary scholars have a more nuanced view of the white philanthropists, observing that their religious convictions came together with their entrepreneurial mentalities to earn money (Anderson and Moss, 1999).

Today this issue of philanthropists' power might be even greater cause for concern given the size of some foundations and the tactics they use. For example, Ravitch (2010), while looking at K–12 education, was critical of venture philanthropists who, through their personal foundations, have helped set education policy through their gifts. Calling them "the Billionaire Boys' Club," Ravitch looked particularly at the philanthropy of the Gates, Walton Family, and Broad foundations. Particularly looking at the Bill and Melinda Gates Foundation, she argued that Gates is involved in setting education policy at all levels—from school districts to the U.S. Department of Education—but that since the foundation is outside the government, it is accountable to no one. Further, she pointed out that "never before was there a foundation that gave grants to almost every major think tank and advocacy group in the field of education, leaving almost no one willing to criticize its vast power and unchecked influence" (p. 211).

By understanding many of the critiques of philanthropy, higher education leaders and scholars will be able to think more critically about the potential impact of decisions to accept gifts and the reliance on philanthropy. Philanthropy has a great power in a college and university context. One should always be mindful, however, of the complexity of the motives with which donations are made.

Conclusion and Challenges for Future Research

> True generosity must benefit both parties. No woman can control her destiny if she doesn't give to herself as much as she gives of herself.
>
> —Suze Orman [National Philanthropic Trust, n.d.]

PHILANTHROPY AND FUNDRAISING have been part of American higher education from its inception. The additive value of voluntary gifts of dollars and time given by alumni, parents, friends, foundations, and corporations to our nation's colleges and universities will never be fully quantified. Although philanthropy research has long been part of the traditional disciplines of economics, psychology, and sociology, it has not been an accepted part of higher education research for very long. In a call for continued research, Hall (1992) noted philanthropic giving is the "single force . . . responsible for the emergence" of American higher education (p. 403). Although Hall was referring to private institutions, perhaps today he would include public higher education. In a recent *New York Times* article, the author noted that private dollars are needed for public higher education to survive in these times of entrenchment. "As state legislatures cut back support for higher education, public colleges and universities across the country are turning to their alumni, hat in hand, as never before—hiring consultants, hunting down graduates, and mobilizing student phone banks to raise private money in amounts they once thought impossible. But many find themselves arriving late to the game. . . . The rush to catch up has placed public campuses in an awkward stance: cutting academic programs and instructors at the same time they are expanding development staffs and investing in a fund-raising infrastructure" (Foderaro, 2011, p. A1). As the need for private dollars increases, the need for more understanding about what motivates alumni and others to give and how colleges and universities cultivate their prospective donors has increased as well.

As with many emerging fields of study, many different opportunities exist for future research. For example, a greater understanding of how colleges and universities help create an engaged citizenry is important. Colleges and university missions often espouse ideals such as creating active and engaged citizens (Hartley and Hollander, 2005; Morphew and Hartley, 2006). The concept, principles, and manifestation of citizenship can take many forms. In *Voices and Equality: Civic Volunteerism in American Politics*, Verba, Schlozman, and Brady (1995) defined voting as the most fundamental act of citizenship with several associated behaviors, including "informal activity in local communities" as relevant to the action. Rimmerman (1997), however, argued that an active and engaged citizen has an expanded role. His definition of engaged citizenship includes broader forms of participation beyond the political realm such as community participation and grassroots mobilization—all forms of volunteerism and philanthropic behaviors.

Although the service-learning and civic engagement literature is vast and expanding (see, for example, Billig, Root, and Jesse, 2005; Colby, Beaumont, Ehrlich, and Corngold, 2007; Colby, Ehrlrich, Beaumont, and Stephens, 2003; Eyler and Giles, 1999), none of the research uses prosocial behavior theory as a framework to examine students' motivations in service learning and the role of universities in the development of students' decisions to volunteer their time. The theoretical frameworks used to understand philanthropic motivations can be useful in this research. Because a link exists between community engagement and increased interest in supporting one's alma mater at HBCUs (Drezner, 2008, 2009, 2010), this work could be very valuable as institutions think about how to cultivate current students to be engaged and active alumni.

Further, a better understanding of how to engage nontraditional donors is needed. As discussed throughout this monograph, traditional fundraising programs at colleges and universities are geared toward wealthy white men. Having a better understanding, from practice and research, of how alumni of color, women, and members of the lesbian, gay, bisexual, transgender, queer, questioning, and intersex communities think about their support of higher education is important so that institutions can begin to engage in more culturally sensitive fundraising practices.

Although a growing body of literature looks at philanthropy and fundraising in nonwhite wealthy male communities (much of it reviewed in this monograph), placing this research in the higher education context is necessary. Much of the current research looks more generally at giving to the nonprofit sector. Many communities view giving to education differently from giving to third-sector organizations such as religion, health, the arts, and the environment.

Research looking at philanthropy's effect on a university's mission is necessary. What effect, if any, do donors, especially those making transformational gifts of tens of millions of dollars, have on university missions? Equally interesting and beneficial is research looking at how colleges' and universities' fundraising efforts and success change as institutional missions evolve. For example, when a single-sex college has chosen to be coeducational, what are the effects on giving? How have those institutions communicated the change of mission to alumni and friends?

Although some work is emerging from doctoral dissertations regarding the role of trustees and senior university leadership with regard to philanthropic support, much remains to be learned. What is the most effective way to engage trustees, presidents, and deans in fundraising? What types of training is needed for these nonprofessional fundraisers? What effects does the increased demand on these positions, with regard to fundraising, have on other institutional governance issues?

Prosocial behaviors can be learned through discussion and direct action. With the increase in academic programs looking at philanthropic studies and nonprofit management across the country, will students' prosocial behaviors increase in the future? Longitudinal studies following students and alumni of these programs will be valuable in understanding the learning of philanthropic behaviors.

Additional research on philanthropy toward colleges and universities among different generations is important. Understanding the formative aspects of graduates' time on campus as well as the larger context of influence on society has not been explored to a great extent. Alumni who were on campus during the 1960 and 1970 protests often look at universities differently from those who graduated during the 1950s. And how do the Millennials think about commitments to their alma mater after graduation?

Still, myriad questions remain. Generally, both qualitative and quantitative work in this regard is needed. The voices of alumni are needed to understand the details of the quantitative studies looking at giving and vice versa. This work is particularly important, as the decision to give voluntary support—in service or monetary contributions—often cannot be fully explained through traditional survey methods.

Although a need exists for more scholarly research by graduate students, faculty, and scholar-practitioners on philanthropy and fundraising in higher education, members of the larger higher education scholarly community must acknowledge this line of inquiry. As mentioned, for too long many claimed that the study of philanthropy and fundraising in higher education is not central to the understanding of postsecondary education. It is not the case, and this monograph attempts to address this concern. At major education research conferences, few philanthropy papers are accepted, and the few presenters are often marginalized to the first or last session of the conference in an out-of-the-way location.

Those of us who study philanthropy or might choose to in the future must therefore make a strong case for the centralization of our study in the education community. Philanthropy was once used exclusively as a margin of excellence for American higher education. Today, it is central to the mere existence and daily function of academe. Where would we be if all current voluntary support and funds derived from past philanthropic giving were all removed from our institutions? As a community of scholars, we must continue to expand our knowledge and understanding of philanthropy so that our institutions, and others, can continue to benefit from its power. The way to do so is by encouraging and supporting both scholarly and scholar-practitioner research that bridges theory and practice.

Perhaps the upside of the current economic downturn—program reductions, furloughs, and retrenchment—is that scholars, administrators, and legislators are more likely to think about the centrality of philanthropy and fundraising to academe. It is my hope that this monograph, which provides an overview of philanthropy's effect on higher education and a review of the theoretical frameworks that guide our research, helps centralize this body of research in the higher education community.

Notes

1. See also the *New Directions in Philanthropic Fundraising* series, Autumn 1993 through Winter 2005 at Wiley Online Library, http://online library.wiley.com/journal/10.1002/(ISSN)1542–7846.

2. LGBTQQI is an inclusive term for sexual minorities and includes lesbian, gay, bisexual, transgender, queer, questioning, and intersex individiusls.

3. The $78 billion figure was calculated using Havens and Schervish's (1999) $6 trillion estimate, assuming that the percentage of all philanthropic giving to education, which is fairly consistent at 13 percent, does not fluctuate over the coming half century.

4. For this chapter, I use "African American" and "black" interchangeably, as much of the literature does not differentiate between the African American and other black communities.

5. The 1992 Survey of Giving and Volunteering in the United States was collected by the Gallup Organization and the Independent Sector.

6. A version of this section was previously written by Noah D. Drezner and published by the Association of Fundraising Professionals. The original article can be found at http://www.afpnet.org/ResourceCenter/ArticleDetail .cfm?ItemNumber=4572.

7. The rest of this book looked exclusively at philanthropy and fundraising from individuals, as individual giving is the dominant source of voluntary support. This chapter broadens the discussion to include philanthropy from corporations and foundations, for such critiques can inform views on individual giving.

8. It should be noted that Levy writes from an Australian perspective and that the tax and entitlement structure is different from that in the United States.

Appendix A: Fundraising Mechanics

The Mechanics of the Annual Fund

As discussed in the first chapter, an annual fund is a significant component of fundraising efforts in higher education. The annual fund provides current-use dollars to institutional operating budgets and is used as a means to cultivate donors for more significant future gifts.

Annual funds solicit donors in multiple ways: personal solicitations, direct mail, phone solicitations, special events, and more recently, e-solicitations. Annual fund solicitations, other than personal solicitations, are characterized as mass appeals that typically combine the "Ask," the "Negotiation" (or the request for multiple different levels of participation, if necessary), and the "Close" of a solicitation in one single transaction (Schroeder, 2002). Kelly (1991) calls this type of e-solicitation or direct mail "asymmetrical," as no interaction occurs between individuals.

Although most annual fund appeals are mass solicitations, the most successful annual funds involve a level of personalization that engages prospective donors. This personalization, beyond the ease of using the prospect's name, is done through segmentation. Alumni and other perspective donor lists can be segmented in a variety of ways based on data the institution has collected. For example, splitting the lists by class year to ask for gifts in honor of a reunion year is standard practice. Others might segment lists by majors or cocurricular activities. For example, a college of education letter to those who studied teacher education might focus on different aspects of the college than a letter appealing to those who graduated from a higher education administration—or student affairs—focused program. Similarly, letters to former scholarship recipients asking for gifts designated for scholarships based on benefits from prior alumni support typically are effective. This segmentation often goes beyond written appeals and can be used in phone solicitations as well.

An Emerging Idea for the Annual Fund

More recently some institutions have asked for multiyear commitments of unrestricted funds. Although this approach contradicts the annual fund norm of requesting support once a year, these programs have been successful in securing larger gifts that institutions can regularly rely on when budgeting for future years. Additionally, as annual fund solicitations often take considerable time, effort, and budget, multiyear requests might help mitigate these considerations (Thompson, Katz, and Briechle, 2010). The University of Rochester found that its multiyear annual fund program (known as the George Eastman Circle, after the university's largest benefactor) helped shield the university in the current economic downturn. Thompson, Katz, and Briechle (2010) found that donors were willing to fulfill prior commitments even if they were unlikely to make new ones. At the height of the economic downturn and the close of fiscal year 2009, the University of Rochester's annual fund grew a remarkable 12.3 percent over the prior year, and the default rate on George Eastman Circle pledges was less than 5 percent (Thompson, Katz, and Briechle, 2010). Innovative approaches to annual giving are becoming more popular and critical to building the pipeline of donors for successful advancement programs.

Planned Giving Instruments

Charitable gift annuities are contracts between a donor and a nonprofit (in this case a higher education institution) that allow the donor to make a gift to the college or university and receive an income for the rest of the donor's life and, if desired, that of one other beneficiary, usually a spouse or partner. The annuity payments and rates depend on the age of the donor and other beneficiary and are based on whether one or two annuitants are named. One variation of the charitable gift annuity is a deferred gift annuity, whereby the income is received at a later date and therefore at a higher annuity rate than the standard charitable gift annuity. An added advantage is that there are no estate taxes if the donor is the only recipient. The principle then reverts to the college or university.

Charitable remainder trusts may be established before or at a donor's death; they pay income to beneficiaries of the donor's choosing for the rest of their life, or a term of twenty years or less, whichever is shorter. The remaining principal from trust goes irrevocably to the college or university. Typically, the annual payout is negotiated when the trust is created; it can range from 5 to 50 percent of the donated amount. The donor names a trustee (a bank, college, or university, for example) and any number of beneficiaries. Charitable remainder trusts avoid capital gains taxes at the time they are created, but tax is still levied on the income payments.

The opposite of charitable remainder trusts, *charitable lead trusts* pay income to the college or university and after a predetermined number of years or the death of donor, the remainder is returned to the donor or his or her heirs. The typical advantage of a charitable lead trust is that it can help transfer wealth from one generation to the next if the heir is in another generation. These transfers are typically at a reduced tax rate compared with estate and gift taxes. In some cases, these trusts can be tax free.

Another possible instrument is *pooled income funds,* which are similar to a mutual fund, whereby the donor's gift is invested in the fund, often the institution's endowment, and the donor receives income for life. The donor may claim a charitable deduction at the time of the gift, however. Pooled income gifts are typically smaller than other types of planned gifts. Upon the donor's death, the "shares" of income fund revert to the college or university.

The simplest planned giving instrument is a *deferred gift* or a *bequest*. Three types of bequests are possible: a specific bequest, in which donors specify in their last will and testament that they are giving the institution a specific dollar amount, number of shares of stock, or even a painting or house; a percentage of the net or gross estate; and a residue of the estate (or percentage of residue).

Donor-Advised Funds

Another giving instrument that some institutions offer through their planned giving office is *donor-advised funds*. Donor-advised funds are a charitable giving vehicle similar to a personal or family foundation in which the principal gift is invested in a pooled fund but is administered by a third party (which can be a for-profit investment firm such as Fidelity or Vanguard or the higher education institution itself). These funds are created for the purpose of managing philanthropic donations on behalf of an organization, family, or individual. A donor-advised fund offers the opportunity to create an easy-to-establish, low-cost, flexible vehicle for philanthropic giving as an alternative to direct giving or creating a private foundation. Donors distribute at least 5 percent of the fund's annual income to any nonprofit, including the higher education institution. If the donor-advised fund is managed by the college or university, the institution typically requires a minimum annual gift to the university based on the returns. Donors enjoy administrative convenience, cost savings, and tax advantages at the time of establishing the fund rather than when annual grants are distributed.

A Caution About Planned Giving

James (2010) cautions that bequests are tricky and might not always garner the funds that the institution or the donor intended. In a study of tens of thousands of Americans over the age of fifty, 4.5 percent indicated that they intended to give charitable donations through bequests. James found that upon that population's death, 59 percent generated no charitable transfers. He explains this significant discrepancy as the result of complex trust and estate laws. Many of those who intended to bequest a portion of their estate to nonprofits might not have realized that much of their estate had transferred to other surviving relatives upon their death, leaving the probate portion of their estate essentially at zero and therefore leaving the nonprofit with nothing or much less than the donor and the institution might have believed:

> *For donors who do not use a living trust, it is important to recognize the difference between the donor's estate and the donor's probate*

estate. . . . Fundraisers may consider encouraging donors to rephrase
percentage bequests. Donors who want to leave 10 percent of their
net worth may consider bequeathing "a dollar amount equal to 10
percent of my adjusted gross estate for federal estate tax purposes." The
adjusted gross estate is the total value of the donor's assets minus debts
and administration costs. . . . However, if a will leaves "10 percent of
my estate," this usually means 10 percent of the probate estate. When
the probate estate is much smaller than the donor's net worth, this
wording change can alter the gift dramatically [James, 2010, p. 12].

For this reason it is very important that both the institution and donor review planned bequests. Should an institution base its budgeting on a bequest that never materializes or is much smaller than predicted, it could encounter serious financial issues.

Appendix B: Philanthropic Research Resources

A growing number of academic centers are focused on the study of philanthropy and the nonprofit sector, including Boston College's Social Welfare Research Institute, Case Western Reserve University's Mandel Center for Nonprofit Organizations, the City University of New York's Center on Philanthropy and Civil Society, Duke University's Center for the Study of Philanthropy and Voluntarism, Grand Valley State University's Dorothy A. Johnson Center for Philanthropy and Nonprofit Leadership, Harvard University's Hauser Center for Nonprofit Institutions, and Indiana University's Center on Philanthropy. Additionally, Indiana University recently established the first bachelor's and Ph.D. programs in philanthropic studies.

Associations and Organizations

American Association of Fundraising Counsel: Giving USA, the annual report on philanthropy, is published by Giving USA Foundation, a public service initiative of the Trust for Philanthropy of the American Association of Fundraising Counsel (AAFRC). The study is researched and written at the Center on Philanthropy at Indiana University. www.AAFRC.org

Aspen Institute: The Aspen Institute's Nonprofit Sector and Philanthropy Program seeks to expand knowledge of the nonprofit sector and philanthropy through research and dialogue focused on public policy management and other important issues affecting the sector. www.aspeninstitute.org

Association of Fundraising Professionals: The AFP represents more than 30,000 members in 213 chapters throughout the world, working to advance philanthropy through advocacy, research, education, and certification programs. The association fosters development and growth of fundraising professionals and promotes high ethical standards in the fundraising profession. www.afpnet.org

Association for Research on Nonprofit Organizations and Voluntary Action: Founded in 1971 as the Association of Voluntary Action Scholars, the ARNOVA is a neutral open forum committed to strengthening the research community in the emerging field of nonprofit and philanthropic studies. The ARNOVA brings together theoretical and applied interests, helping scholars gain insight into the day-to-day concerns of third-sector organizations while providing nonprofit professionals with research they can use to improve the quality of life for citizens and communities. Principal activities include an annual conference, publications, electronic discussions, and special interest groups. www.arnova.org

Boston College Center on Wealth and Philanthropy: The CWP is a multidisciplinary research center specializing in the study of spirituality, wealth, philanthropy, and other aspects of cultural life in an age of affluence. www.bc.edu/swri

Center for Effective Philanthropy: The center pursues its mission through data collection and research that fuel the creation of assessment tools, publications, and programming and recognition. Since receiving initial funding in 2001, the center has produced widely referenced research reports on foundation performance assessment, foundation governance, and foundation-grantee relationships. www.effectivephilanthropy.org

Center on Philanthropy at Indiana University: The Center on Philanthropy at Indiana University is a leading academic center dedicated to increasing the understanding of philanthropy and improving its practice through research, teaching, public service and public affairs. The center focuses on increasing knowledge about the nonprofit or philanthropic sector and improving the practices of giving, fundraising, nonprofit organization management, and other aspects of philanthropic activity. www.philanthropy.iupui.edu

City University of New York Center on Philanthropy and Civil Society: The center is committed to strengthening civil society through education, research, and leadership training. www.philanthropy.org

Council for Advancement and Support of Education: The CASE helps its members build stronger relationships with their alumni and donors, raise funds for campus projects, produce recruitment materials, market their institutions to prospective students, diversify the profession, and foster public support of education. www.case.org

Council for Aid to Education: The CAE is a national nonprofit organization established to advance corporate support of education and to conduct policy research on higher education. Today the CAE is also focused on improving quality and access in higher education. The CAE is the nation's sole source of empirical data on private giving to education through the annual Voluntary Support of Education survey and its Data Miner interactive database. www.cae.org

Foundation Center: Established in 1956 and today supported by close to 550 foundations, the Foundation Center is the leading source of information about philanthropy worldwide. Through data, analysis, and training it connects people who want to change the world to the resources they need to succeed. The center maintains the most comprehensive database on U.S. and, increasingly, global grant makers and their grants—a robust, accessible knowledge bank for the sector. It also operates research, education, and training programs designed to advance knowledge of philanthropy at every level. The center's clients are served in its five regional library and learning centers and its network of 450 funding information centers located in public libraries, community foundations, and educational institutions. www.foundationcenter.org

Independent Sector: The Independent Sector is committed to strengthening, empowering, and partnering with nonprofit and philanthropic organizations in their work on behalf of the public good. www.independentsector.org

National Association of College and Business Officers: The NACUBO represents chief administrative and financial officers through a collaboration of knowledge and professional development, advocacy, and community. The organization publishes an annual Study of Endowments with Commonfund. www.nacubo.org

National Center for Charitable Statistics: The NCCS, a program of the Center on Nonprofits and Philanthropy at the Urban Institute, is the national clearinghouse of data on the nonprofit sector in the United States. www.nccs.urban.org

New York University School of Law National Center on Philanthropy and the Law: The NCPL was established to explore a broad range of legal issues affecting the nation's nonprofit sector and to provide an integrated examination of the legal doctrines related to the activities of charitable organizations. www.law.nyu.edu/ncpl

Partnership for Philanthropic Planning: The partnership helps to maximize the value of charitable giving for nonprofit organizations and donors by helping fundraising professionals provide the most meaningful charitable giving experience for donors, helping financial planning professionals provide their clients with excellent advice on charitable giving and estate planning, and helping nonprofit managers and trustees better accomplish the missions of their organizations through meaningful philanthropic planning. www.pppnet.org

Planned Giving Design Center: The center is a national network of hosting organizations that provide members with timely, objective content on charitable taxation and planned giving, an engaging community, and a collection of services aimed at facilitating charitable gifts. www.pgdc.com/usa

University of Southern California Center on Philanthropy and Public Policy: USC's Center on Philanthropy and Public Policy promotes more effective philanthropy and strengthens the nonprofit sector through research that informs philanthropic decision making and public policy to advance public problem solving. www.usc.edu/schools/sppd/philanthropy

Peer-Reviewed Journals

Nonprofit and Voluntary Sector Quarterly, published bimonthly, is an international, interdisciplinary journal for nonprofit sector research dedicated to enhancing knowledge of nonprofit organizations, philanthropy, and volunteerism by providing cutting-edge research, discussion, and analysis of the field. *NVSQ* provides a forum for researchers from around the world to publish timely articles from a variety of disciplinary perspectives.

The *NVSQ* is sponsored by the Association for Research on Nonprofit Organizations and Voluntary Action. nvs.sagepub.com

Voluntas: International Journal of Voluntary and Nonprofit Organizations, the journal of the International Society for Third-Sector Research (ISTR), is a major international association promoting research and education in the fields of civil society, philanthropy, and the nonprofit sector. The ISTR is an organization committed to building a global community of scholars and interested others dedicated to the creation, discussion, and advancement of knowledge pertaining to the Third Sector and its impact on human and planetary well-being and development internationally. www.istr.org/pubs/voluntas/index.htm. www.springerlink.com/content/ 0957-8765

The International Journal of Education Advancement publishes new ideas, shares examples of best practices, and develops a body of knowledge in educational advancement. The journal includes articles from academic researchers and advancement professionals working in schools, colleges, and universities; thus providing a forum for the equally important aspects of alumni relations, fundraising, communications, public relations, and marketing. Its content acknowledges the increasingly complex management of advancement with in-depth articles and cutting-edge analysis of new concepts and applications. www.palgrave-journals.com/ijea/index.html

Other Publications

Chronicle of Philanthropy
www.philanthropy.com

Fundraising Success Magazine
www.fundraisingsuccessmag.com

Non-Profit Times
www.nptimes.com

Philanthropy Journal Online
www.philanthropyjournal.org

Philanthropy News Digest
www.fdncenter.org/pnd

Philanthropy Roundtable
philanthropyroundtable.org

Planned Giving Today
www.pgtoday.com

Databases

Catalog of Nonprofit Literature is a searchable database of the literature of philanthropy. Incorporating the contents of the Foundation Center's five
libraries, it contains approximately 28,000 full bibliographic citations,
nearly 20,000 of which have descriptive abstracts. It is updated daily. The
catalog was formerly known as Literature of the Nonprofit Sector.
cnl.foundationcenter.org

The Philanthropic Studies Index is a tool for locating information about volunteerism, nonprofit organizations, fundraising, and charitable giving. The
bulk of citations currently indexed are from academic journals, dated 1940
to the present. It also includes some dissertations, working papers, web
sites, and other information sources. cheever.ulib.iupui.edu/psipublisearch

Voluntary Support of Education Survey
The Council for Aid to Education's Voluntary Support of Education Survey
is the authoritative national source of information on private giving to
higher education and private K–12 schools, consistently capturing about
85 percent of the total voluntary support to colleges and universities in
the United States. The CAE has managed the survey as a public service
for more than fifty years. www.cae.org/content/pro_data_trends.htm

Other Useful Resources

Association of Fundraising Professionals: The AFP fosters the development and growth of fundraising professionals and the profession, promotes high ethical standards in the fundraising profession through its Standards of Professional Practice, and preserves and enhances philanthropy and volunteerism. www.afpnet.org/Ethics

Council for Advancement and Support of Education: The CASE Management and Reporting Standards provide a common set of definitions and procedures for managing and reporting the results of fundraising activities at educational institutions. www.case.org

References

Ahammer, I. M., and Murray, J. P. (1979). Kindness in the kindergarten: The relative influence of role playing and prosocial television in facilitating altruism. *International Journal of Behavioral Development, 2,* 133–157.

Albert, S., and Whetten, D. A. (1985). Organizational identity. In L. L. Cummings and B. M. Staw (Eds.), *Research in organizational behavior.* (Vol. 7, pp. 263–295). Greenwich, CT: JAI Press.

Alperovitz, G. (2005). *America beyond capitalism: Reclaiming our Wealth, our Liberty, and our democracy.* Hoboken, NJ: Wiley.

American Association of Fundraising Counsel. (2003). *Giving USA 2003: The annual report on philanthropy for the year 2002.* New York: American Association of Fundraising Counsel.

Anderson, E., and Moss, A. (1999). *Dangerous donations: White northern philanthropy and black education.* Columbia: University of Missouri Press.

Anderson, J. D. (1988). *The education of blacks in the South.* Chapel Hill: University of North Carolina Press.

Andreoni, J. (1988). Privately provided public goods in a large economy: The limits of altruism. *Journal of Public Economics, 35,* 57–73.

Andreoni, J. (1989). Giving with impure altruism: Applications to charity and Ricardian equivalence. *Journal of Public Economy, 97*(6), 1447–1458.

Andreoni, J. (1990). Impure altruism and donations to public goods: A theory of warm-glow giving. *Economic Journal, 100*(401), 464–477.

Andreoni, J. (1998). Toward a theory of charitable fund-raising. *Journal of Political Economy, 160*(6), 1186–1213.

Andreoni, J., Brown, E., and Rischall, I. (2003). Charitable giving by married couples: Who decides and why does it matter? *Journal of Human Resources, 38*(1), 111–133.

Anft, M., and Lipman, H. (2003). How Americans give: Chronicle study finds that race is a powerful influence. *Chronicle on Philanthropy, 15*(14).

Apinunmahakul, A., and Devlin, R. A. (2004). Charitable giving and charitable gambling: An empirical investigation. *National Tax Journal, 57,* 67–88.

Arnove, R. F. (1980a). Comparative education and world-systems analysis. *Comparative Education Review, 24*(1), 48–62.

Arnove, R. F. (Ed.). (1980b). *Philanthropy and cultural imperialism: The foundations at home and abroad.* Bloomington: Indiana University Press.

Ascoli, P. (2006). *Julius Rosenwald: The man who Built Sears, Roebuck, and advanced the cause of black education in the American south.* Bloomington: Indiana University Press.

Ashcraft, R. F. (1995). An analysis of alumni donation and nondonation related to selected personal, involvement and outcome factors. Unpublished Ph.D. dissertation, Arizona State University.

Ashforth, B. E., and Mael, F. (1989). Social identity theory and the organization. *Academy of Management Review, 14*, 20–39.

Astin, A. W., and Sax, L. J. (1998). How undergraduates are affected by service participation. *Journal of College Student Development, 39*, 251–263.

Astin, A. W., Sax, L. J., and Avalos, J. (2008). Long-term effects of volunteerism during the undergraduate years. In A. Walton and others (Eds.), *Philanthropy, volunteerism and fundraising in higher education* (pp. 389–399). Upper Saddle River, NJ: Pearson.

Atchley, R. C. (1989). A continuity theory of normal aging. *Gerontologist, 29*(2), 183–190.

Avery, R. (1994). The pending intergenerational wealth transfer. *Philanthropy, 3*(1), 28–29.

Banks, J., and Tanner, S. (1999). Patterns in household giving: Evidence from UK data. *International Journal of Voluntary and Nonprofit Organizations, 10*, 167–178.

Bar-Tal, D. (1976). *Prosocial behavior.* Washington, DC: Hemisphere Publishing Company.

Bar-Tal, D. (1982). Sequential development of helping behavior: A cognitive-learning approach. *Developmental Review, 2*, 101–124.

Becker, G. S. (1974). A theory of social interactions. *Journal of Political Economy, 82*(6), 1063–1093.

Becker, G. S. (1976). *The economic approach to human behavior.* Chicago: University of Chicago Press.

Bekkers, R. (2003). Volunteering from one generation to the next: Modeling effects or confounding variables? Mimeo, Utrect University.

Bekkers R. (2004). Giving and volunteering in the Netherlands: Sociological and psychological perspectives. Ph.D. dissertation, Department of Sociology, Utrecht University, The Netherlands.

Bekkers, R. (2006). Traditional and health related philanthropy: The role of resources and personality. *Social Psychology Quarterly, 68*, 349–366.

Bekkers, R., and De Graaf, N. D. (2006). Education and prosocial behavior. Manuscript, Utrecht University, The Netherlands.

Bekkers, R., and Wiepking, P. (2007). Generosity and philanthropy: A literature review. Unpublished manuscript. Retrieved September 15, 2008, from http://papers.ssrn.com/sol3/papers.cfm?abstract_id=1015507.

Belfield, C. R., and Beney, A. P. (2000). What determines alumni generosity? Evidence for the UK. *Education Economics, 8*, 65–80.

Bentley, R. J., and Nissan, L. G. (1996). *The roots of giving and serving.* Indianapolis: Indiana University Center on Philanthropy.

Bergstrom, T. C., Blume, L., and Varian, H. (1986). On the private provision of public goods. *Journal of Public Economics, 29,* 25–49.

Berman, E. (1980a). Educational colonialism in Africa: The role of American foundations, 1910–1945. In R. F. Arnove (Ed.), *Philanthropy and cultural imperialism: The foundations at home.* Boston: G. K. Hall.

Berman, E. (1980b). The foundations' role in American foreign policy: The case of Africa, post-1945. In R. F. Arnove (Ed.), *Philanthropy and cultural imperialism: The foundations at home.* Boston: G.K. Hall.

Berman, E. (1982). The extension of ideology: Foundation support for intermediate organizations and forums. *Comparative Education Review, 26*(1), 48–68.

Berry, M. L. (1999). Native American philanthropy: Expanding social participation and self-determination. In *Cultures of caring: Philanthropy in diverse American communities.* Washington, DC: Council on Foundations.

Bielefeld, W., Rooney, P., and Steinberg, K. (2005). How do need, capacity, geography, and politics influence giving? In A Brooks (Ed.), *Gifts of money in America's communities* (pp. 127–158). Lanham, MD: Rowman & Littlefield.

Billig, S., Root, S., and Jesse, D. (2005). The impact of participation in service-learning on high school students' civic engagement. Working Paper 33. Center for Information & Research on Civic Learning and Engagement.

Birkholz, J. (2008). *Fundraising analytics: Using data to guide strategy.* Hoboken, NJ: Wiley.

Bjorhovde, P. O. (2002a). *Teaching philanthropy to children: A comprehensive study of philanthropy curricula.* Winona: St. Mary's University of Minnesota.

Bjorhovde, P. O. (2002b). Teaching philanthropy to children: Why, how, and what. In P. O. Bjorhovde (Ed.), Creating tomorrow's philanthropists: Curriculum development for youth. *New Directions for Philanthropic Fundraising, 36,* 7–19.

Blau, P. M. (1992). *Exchange and power in social life* (3rd ed.). New Brunswick, NJ: Transaction Publishers.

Blumenfeld, W. S., and Sartain, P. L. (1974). Predicting alumni financial donations. *Journal of Applied Psychology 59,* 522–523.

Bolton, G. E., and Katok, E. (1995). An experimental test for gender differences in beneficent behavior. *Economic Letters, 48,* 287–292.

Boverini, L. (2006). When venture philanthropy rocks the ivory tower. *International Journal of Educational Advancement, 6,* 84–106.

Bradford, A. (1837). Historical sketch of Harvard University. *Quarterly Register, 9,* 321–366.

Brawley, J. P. (1981). Oral history interview by Marcia Goodson, Columbia University Oral History Collection, New York, NY.

Bremner, R. H. (1996). *Giving: Charity and philanthropy in history.* New Brunswick, NJ: Transaction Publishers.

Briechle, P. (2003). Does institutional type affect alumnae donating patterns in the United States? *International Journal of Educational Advancement, 4*(1), 19–29.

Brittingham, B. E., and Pezzullo, T. R. (1989, November). *Fund raising in higher education: What we know, what we need to know.* Paper presented at the Annual Meeting of the Association of Higher Education, Atlanta, GA. (ED 313 988)

Brittingham, B. E., and Pezzullo, T. R. (1990). *The campus green: Fund raising in higher education.* ASHE-ERIC Higher Education Report (Vol. 19, No. 1). Washington, DC: The George Washington University, School of Education and Human Development.

Broce, T. E. (1986). *Fund raising: The guide to raising money from private sources* (2nd ed.). Norman: University of Oklahoma Press.

Brooks, A. C. (2004). The effects of public policy on private charity. *Administration & Society, 36,* 166–185.

Brown, E. (2005). College, social capital, and charitable giving. In A. Brooks (Ed.), *Gifts of time and money in America's communities.* Lanham, MD: Rowman & Littlefield.

Brown, E., and Ferris, J. M. (2007). Social capital and philanthropy: An analysis of the impact of social capital on individual giving and volunteering. *Nonprofit and Voluntary Sector Quarterly, 36,* 85–99.

Brown, E., and Lankford, H. (1992). Gifts of money and gifts of time: Estimating the effects of tax prices and available time. *Journal of Public Economics, 47*(3), 321–341.

Brown, M. C. (2004). Making the case for corporate philanthropy. In H. P. Karoff (Ed.), *Just money: A critique of contemporary American philanthropy* (pp. 151–164). Boston: TPI Editions.

Brown-Kruse, J., and Hummels, D. (1993). Gender effects in laboratory public goods contributions: Do individuals put their money where their mouth is? *Journal of Economic Behavior and Organization, 22,* 255–268.

Bruggink, T. H., and Siddiqui, K. (1995). An econometric model of alumni giving: A case study for a liberal arts college. *American Economist, 392,* 53–60.

Burgoyne, C. B., Young, B., and Walker, C. M. (2005). Deciding to give to charity: A focus group study in the context of the household economy. *Journal of Community & Applied Social Psychology, 15*(5), 383–405.

Burnett, K. (1992/2002). *Relationship fundraising,* London: White Lion Press.

Butler, S. M. (2001, March 8). Why the Bush tax cuts are no threat to philanthropy. *Heritage Foundation Backgrounder.*

Buttle, F. (1996). Relationship marketing. In F. Buttle (Ed.), *Relationship marketing: Theory and practice.* London: Paul Chapman Publishing.

Byrd, A. (Ed.). (1990). *Philanthropy and the black church.* Washington, DC: Council on Foundations.

Capek, M.E.S. (2001). *Women and philanthropy: Old stereotypes, new challenges – A monograph series.* St. Paul, MN: Women's Funding Network.

Capek, M.E.S., and Mead, M. (2006). *Effective philanthropy: Organizational success through deep diversity and gender equality.* Cambridge: MIT Press.

Carbone, R. F. (1986). *Agenda for research on fund raising* (Monograph No. 1). College Park: Clearinghouse for Research on Fund Raising, University of Maryland.

Carman, K. G. (2006). Social influences and the private provision of public goods: Evidence from charitable contributions in the workplace. Discussion Paper. Stanford, CA: Stanford Institute for Economic Policy Research, Stanford University.

Carroll, J., McCarthy, S., and Newman, C. (2006). An econometric analysis of charitable donations in the Republic of Ireland. *Economic and Social Review, 36,* 229–249.

Carson, E. (1989a, Summer). Black philanthropy: Shaping tomorrow's nonprofit sector. *National Society of Fund Raising Executives Journal*, 23–31.

Carson, E. (1989b). *A charitable appeals fact book: How black and white Americans respond to different types of fund-raising efforts.* Washington DC: Joint Center for Political Studies.

Carson, E. (1990). Patterns of giving in black churches. In V. A. Hodgkinson, R. Wuthnow, and associates (Eds.), *Faith and philanthropy in America: Exploring the role of religion in America's voluntary sector.* San Francisco: Jossey-Bass.

Carson, E. (1993). *A hand up: Black philanthropy and self-help in America.* Washington, DC: Joint Center for Political Studies.

Cascione, G. L. (2003). *Philanthropists in higher education: Institutional, biographical, and religious motivations for giving.* New York: Routledge Falmer.

Center on Philanthropy and Civil Society. (2004). *African American philanthropy literature review.* New York: Center on Philanthropy and Civil Society.

Chang, W-C. (2005). Religious giving, non-religious giving, and after-life consumption. *Topics in Economic Analysis and Policy, 5*(1), 1421.

Chao, J. (1999). Asian American philanthropy: Expanding circles of participation. In *Cultures of caring philanthropy in diverse American communities.* Washington DC: Council on Foundations.

Chao, J. (2002/2008). What is Chinese American philanthropy? In A. Walton and others (Eds.), *Philanthropy, volunteerism and fundraising in higher education* (pp. 816–818). Boston: Pearson.

Chernow, R. (2004). *Titan: The life of John D. Rockefeller, Sr.* New York: Knopf.

Chewning, P. B. (1993). The ultimate goal: Installing the volunteer and philanthropic ethic. In B. T. Todd (Ed.), *Student advancement programs: Shaping tomorrow's leaders today.* Washington, DC: Council for the Advancement and Support of Education.

Chua, V.C.H., and Wong, C. M. (1999). Tax incentives, individual characteristics and charitable giving in Singapore. *International Journal of Social Economics, 26,* 1492–1504.

Cialdini, R. B., and Kenrick, D. T. (1976). Altruism as hedonism: A social development perspective on the relationship of negative mood state helping. *Journal of Personality and Social Psychology, 34,* 907–914.

Ciconte, B. K., and Jacob, J. G. (2001). *Fund raising basics: A complete guide.* Sudbury, MA: Jones & Bartlett.

Clark, M. S. (1992). Research on communal and exchange relationships viewed from a functionalist perspective. In D. A. Owens and M. Wagner (Eds.), *Progress in modern psychology: The legacy of American functionalism* (pp. 241–258). Westport , CT: Praeger.

Clary, E. G., and Snyder, M. (1990). *A functional analysis of volunteers' motivations.* Paper presented at a meeting of the Spring Research Forum, Boston.

Colby, A., Beaumont, E., Ehrlich, T., and Corngold, J. (2007). *Educating for democracy: Preparing undergraduates for responsible political engagement.* San Francisco: Jossey- Bass.

Colby, A., Ehrlich, T., Beaumont, E., and Stephens, J. (2003). *Educating citizens: Preparing America's undergraduates for lives of moral and civic responsibility.* San Francisco: Jossey-Bass.

Community Foundation for Greater Atlanta. (2004). *African American philanthropy in metro Atlanta.* Atlanta: Community Foundation for Greater Atlanta.

Conley, D. (2000). The racial wealth gap: Origins and implications for philanthropy in the African American community. *Nonprofit and Voluntary Sector Quarterly, 29*(4), 530.

Connolly, M. S., and Blanchette, R. (1986). Understanding and predicting alumni giving behavior. In J. A. Dunn (Ed.), *New directions for institutional research: Enhancing the management of fund raising.* (Volume 51, pp. 69–89). San Francisco: Jossey-Bass.

Connors, T. D. (2001). *The nonprofit handbook* (3rd ed). New York: Wiley.

Cook, W. B., and Lasher, W. F. (1996). Toward a theory of fund raising in higher education. *Review of Higher Education, 20*(1), 33–51.

Cornes, R., and Sandler, T. (1984). Easy riders, joint production, and public goods. *Economic Journal, 94*(375), 580–598.

Council for Aid to Education. (2004). Voluntary support of education survey. Retrieved April 14, 2005, from http://vse.cae.org.

Council for Aid to Education. (2010). *Voluntary Support of Education 2009.* Retrieved December 1, 2010, from http://vse.cae.org

Council for Aid to Education. (1973). *Volunteerism, Tax Reform, and Higher Education.* Author, New York.

Council on Foundations. (1999). *Cultures of caring: Philanthropy in diverse American communities.* Washington, DC: Council on Foundations.

Cox, J. C., and Deck, C. A. (2006). When are women more generous than men? *Economic Inquiry, 44*(4), 587–598.

Croson, R., and Buchan, N. (1999). Gender and culture: International experimental evidence from trust games. *American Economic Review, 89,* 386–391.

Curti, M., and Nash, R. (1965). *Philanthropy in the shaping of American higher education.* New Brunswick, NJ: Rutgers University Press.

Cutlip, S. M. (1965). *Fund raising in the United States.* New Brunswick, NJ: Rutgers University Press.

Daloz, L. P. (1998). Can generosity be taught? *Essays on philanthropy (No. 29).* Indianapolis: Indiana University Center on Philanthropy.

Dalzell, R., and Dalzell, L. (2007). *The house the Rockefellers built: A tale of money, taste, and power in twentieth century America.* New York: Henry Holt.

Davis, K. E. (1975). *Fundraising in the Black community: History, feasibility, and conflict.* Metuchen, NJ: Scarecrow Press.

Dawes, R., Van de Kragt, J.C.A., and Orbell, J. M. (1990). Cooperation for the benefit of us—not me or my conscience. In J. J. Mansbridge (Ed.), *Beyond self-interest* (pp. 97–110). Chicago: University of Chicago Press.

de la Garza, R., and Lu, F. (1999). Explorations into Latino voluntarism. In *Nuevos senderos: Reflections on Hispanics and philanthropy* (pp. 55–78). Houston: Arte Publico Press.

Desruisseaux, P. (1985, April 10). Non-profit sector is now a hot topic for researchers in several fields. *Chronicle of Higher Education, 18.*

Diamond, W. D., and Kashyap, R. K. (1997). Extending models of prosocial behavior to explain university alumni contributions. *Journal of Applied Social Psychology, 27*(10), 915–928.

Dove, K. E. (2001). *Conducting a successful fundraising program: A comprehensive guide and resource.* San Francisco: Jossey-Bass.

Drezner, N. D. (2005). Advancing Gallaudet: Alumni support for the nation's university for the deaf and hard-of-hearing and its similarities to black colleges and universities. *International Journal of Educational Advancement, 5*(4), 301–315.

Drezner, N. D. (2006). Recessions and tax cuts: The impact of economic cycles on individual giving, philanthropy, and higher education. *International Journal of Educational Advancement, 6*(4), 289–305.

Drezner, N. D. (2008). For alma mater and the fund: The United Negro College Fund's National Pre-Alumni Council and the creation of the next generation of donors. In M. Gasman and C. Tudico (Eds.), *Triumphs and troubles: Historical and contemporary essays on black colleges.* New York: Palgrave Macmillan.

Drezner, N. D. (2009). Why give? Exploring social exchange and organizational identification theories in the promotion of philanthropic behaviors of African American millennials at private HBCUs. *International Journal of Educational Advancement, 9*(3), 147–165.

Drezner, N. D. (2010). Prosocial behavior development: The case of private black colleges encouraging student philanthropic giving and volunteerism. *International Journal of Educational Advancement, 10*(3), 126–147.

Dugan, K., Mullin, C., and Siegfried, J. (2000). Undergraduate financial aid and subsequent giving behavior. Williams Project on the Economics of Higher Education Discussion Papers (DP-57). Williams, MA: Williams College.

Duncan, B. (1999). Modeling charitable contributions of time and money. *Journal of Public Economics, 72,* 213–242.

Duncan, B. (2004). A theory of impact philanthropy. *Journal of Public Economics, 88*(9–10), 2159–2180.

Dunlop, D. R. (2002). Major gift programs. In M. J. Worth (Ed.), *New strategies for educational fund raising* (pp. 89–104). Westport, CT: Praeger.

Duronion, M. A., and Loession, B. A. (1991). *Effective fund raising in higher education.* San Francisco: Jossey-Bass.

Eagly, A. H., and Crowley, M. (1986). Gender and helping behavior: A meta-analytic review of the social psychological literature. *Psychological Bulletin, 100,* 283–308.

Eckel, C. C., and Grossman, P. J. (1998). Are women less selfish than men? Evidence from dictator experiments. *Economic Journal, 108,* 726–735.

Eckel, C. C., and Grossman, P. J. (2001). Chivalry and solidarity in ultimatum games. *Economic Inquiry, 39,* 171–187.

Eckel, C. C., and Grossman, P. J. (2003). Rebate versus matching: Does how we subsidize charitable contributions matter? *Journal of Public Economics, 87,* 681–701.

Eckel, C. C., Grossman, P. J., and Johnston, R. M. (2005). An experimental test of the crowding out hypothesis. *Journal of Public Economics, 89,* 1543–1560.

Edwards, M. (2008). *Just another emperor? The myths and realities of philanthrocapitalism.* New York: Young Foundation & Demos.

Einolf, C. J. (2006). The roots of altruism: A gender and life course perspective. Retrieved August 1, 2008, from ProQuest Digital Dissertations http://gradworks.umi.com/32/35/3235030.html.

Eisenburg, N. (Ed.). (1982). *The development of prosocial behavior.* New York: Academic Press.

Eisenberg, N., and Mussen, P. H. (1989). *The roots of prosocial behavior in children.* Cambridge: Cambridge University Press.

Elliott, D. (2006). *The kindness of strangers: Philanthropy and higher education.* Lanham, MD: Rowman & Littlefield.

Ellison, C. G., and Sherkat, D. E. (1995). The semi-involuntary institution revisited: Regional variations in church participation among black Americans. *Social Forces, 73*(4), 1415–1437.

Eschholz, S. L., and Van Slyke, D. M. (2002). *New evidence about women and philanthropy: Findings from metro Atlanta.* Atlanta: Women's Legacy, United Way of Metropolitan Atlanta.

Eyler, J., and Giles, D. E., Jr. (1999). *Where's the learning in service learning?* San Francisco: Jossey-Bass.

Fairfax, J. E. (1995). Black philanthropy: Its heritage and its future. *New Directions for Philanthropic Fundraising* (Volume 6, pp. 9–21). San Francisco: Jossey-Bass.

Feldman, N. E. (2007). Time is money: Choosing between charitable activities. Working paper. Israel: Ben-Gurion University.

Feldstein, M., and Clotfelter, C. T. (1976). Tax incentives and charitable contributions in the United States. *Journal of Public Economics, 5,* 1–26.

Filer Commission on Private Philanthropy and Public Needs. (1975/2004). In D. F. Burlingame (Ed.), *Philanthropy in America: A comprehensive historical encyclopedia* (Volume 3, pp. 742–774). Santa Barbara, CA: ABC-CLIO.

Flanagan, J. (1999). *Successful fundraising: A complete handbook for volunteers and professionals.* New York: McGraw-Hill.

Foderaro, L. W. (2011, January 16). Amid cuts, public colleges step up appeals to alumni. *New York Times,* A1.

Frey B. S., and Meier, S. (2004). Prosocial behavior in a natural setting. *Journal of Economic Behavior & Organization, 54,* 65–88.

Friedmann, A. S. (2003). Building communities of participation through student advancement programs: A first step towards relationship fund raising. (Ph.D. dissertation, College of William and Mary).

Fygetakis, E. C., and Dalton, J. C. (1993). The relationship between student affairs and institutional advancement offices in educational fundraising. *New Directions for Student Services* (Volume 63, pp. 51–61) San Francisco: Jossey-Bass.

Gaier, S. (2005). Alumni satisfaction with their undergraduate academic experiences and the impact on alumni giving and participation. *International Journal of Educational Advancement, 5*(4), 279–288.

Gamble, P. R., Stone, M., and Woodcock, N. (1999). *Up close and personal: Customer relationship marketing @ work.* Dover, NH: Kogan Page.

Garvin, C. C., Jr. (1978). *Corporate philanthropy: The third aspect of social responsibility.* New York: Council for Financial Aid to Education.

Gasman, M. (2001). *Racial stereotyping in fundraising for historically black colleges: A historical case study.* Paper presented at an annual meeting of the American Education Research Association, Seattle, WA. (ED474940)

Gasman, M. (2002). An untapped resource: Bringing African Americans into the college and university giving process. *CASE International Journal of Educational Advancement, 2*(3), 280–292.

Gasman, M. (2003) A word for every occasion: John D. Rockefeller Jr. and the United Negro College Fund. *History of Higher Education Annual,* Transaction Publishers.

Gasman, M. (2004). Rhetoric vs. reality: The fundraising messages of the United Negro College Fund in the immediate aftermath of the *Brown* decision. *History of Education Quarterly, 44*(1), 70–94.

Gasman, M. (2006a). Perspectives: Black colleges must tap alumni support. *Diverse Issues in Higher Education.* Retrieved August 6, 2007, from http://www.diverseeducation.com/artman/publish/article_6087.shtml.

Gasman, M. (2006b). Trends in African American philanthropy. *On Philanthropy.* Retrieved March 3, 2006, from http://www.onphilanthropy.com/site/News2?page=NewsArticle&id=5623.

Gasman, M. (2007). *Envisioning Black colleges: A history of the United Negro College Fund.* Baltimore: Johns Hopkins University Press.

Gasman, M., and Anderson-Thompkins, S. (2003). *Fund raising from Black college alumni: Successful strategies for supporting alma mater.* Washington, DC: Council for the Advancement and Support of Education.

Gasman, M., Beaz, B., and Turner, C.S.V. (2008). *Understanding Minority Serving Institutions.* New York: State University of New York Press.

Gasman, M., and Drezner, N. D. (2007). *A maverick in the field: The Oram Group and fundraising for change in the Black college community during the 1970s.* Paper presented at a meeting of the American Educational Research Association, Chicago, IL.

Gasman, M., and Drezner, N. D. (2008). White corporate philanthropy and its support of private black colleges in the 1960s and 1970s. *International Journal of Educational Advancement, 8*(2), 79–92.

Gasman, M., and Drezner, N. D. (2009). A maverick in the field: The Oram Group and fundraising for change in the black college community during the 1970s. *History of Education Quarterly, 49*(4), 465–506.

Gasman, M., and Drezner, N. D. (2010). Fundraising for black colleges during the 1960s and 1970s: The case of Hampton Institute. *Nonprofit and Voluntary Sector Quarterly, 39*(2), 321–342.

Gasman, M., and others. (2011). *Race and gender in foundation and nonprofit leadership.* New York: Palgrave Macmillan.

Gasman, M., and Sedgwick, K. V. (2005). *Uplifting a people: African American philanthropy and education.* New York: Peter Lang.

"Generation to generation." *New York Times,* Dec. 17, 1937, p. 24.

Giroux, H. A. (1998). Education incorporated? *Educational Leadership, 56*(2), 12–17.

Giving USA. (2010). *The annual report on philanthropy for the year 2009.* New York: *Giving USA.*

Gordon, K. (1975). Foreword. In A. M. Okun (Ed.), *Equality and efficiency: The big tradeoff* (p. 120). Washington, DC: The Brookings Institution.

Greenfield, J. (2001). *The nonprofit handbook: Fund raising.* New York: Wiley.

Grenzebach Glier and Associates. (2010). Completed capital campaigns in higher education with billion-dollar + goals. Chicago: Grenzebach Glier & Associates.

Gruber, J. (2004). Pay or pray? The impact of charitable subsidies on religious attendance. *Journal of Public Economics, 88,* 2635–2655.

Grusec, J. E. (1982). The socialization of altruism. In N. Eisenberg (ed.), *The development of prosocial behavior.* New York: Academic Press.

Grusec, J. E. (1991). The socialization of empathy. In M. S. Clark (Ed.), *Review of personality and social psychology. Volume 12, Prosocial behavior* (pp. 9–33). Newbury Park, CA: Sage.

Grusec, J., and Kuczynski, L. (Eds.). (1997). *Parenting and children's internalization of values: A handbook of contemporary theory.* New York: Wiley.

Hall, P. D. (1992). Teaching and research on philanthropy, voluntarism, and nonprofit organizations: A case study of academic innovation. *Teachers College Record, 93*(3), 403–436.

Hall-Russell, C., and Kasberg, R. H. (1997). *African American traditions of giving and serving: A midwest perspective.* Indianapolis: Center on Philanthropy, Indiana University.

Harbaugh, W. (1998). The prestige motive for making charitable transfers. *American Economics Review Papers and Proceedings, 88*(2), 277–282.

Harrison, W. B. (1995). College relations and fund-raising expenditures: Influencing the probability of alumni giving to higher education. *Economics of Education Review, 14*(1), 73–84.

Hartley, M., and Hollander, E. (2005). The elusive ideal: Civic learning and higher education. In S. Fuhrman and M. Lazerson (Eds.), *The public schools.* The Institutions of American Democracy series. New York: Oxford University Press.

Harvard. (n.d.). *The Harvard Hymn.* Retrieved September 1, 2007, from http://www.math.harvard.edu/history/hymn/.

Havens, J. (1994). *Giving behavior by income and gender: Do men give more?* Boston: Social Welfare Research Institute, Boston College.

Havens, J. J., and Schervish, P. G. (1999). Millionaires and the millennium: New estimates of the forthcoming wealth transfer and the prospects for a golden age of philanthropy. Boston: Social Welfare Research Institute, Boston College.

Havens, J. J., and Schervish, P. G. (2003). Why the $41 trillion wealth transfer estimate is still valid: A review of challenges and questions. *Journal of Gift Planning, 7*(1), 11–15.

Havens, J. J., and Schervish, P. G. (2005). Wealth transfer estimates for African American households. *New Directions for Philanthropic Fundraising, 48*, 47–55.

Higginbotham, E. B. (1993). *Righteous discontent: The women's movement in the black Baptist church, 1880–1920.* Cambridge, MA: Harvard University Press.

Hillygus, D. S. (2005). The missing link: Exploring the relationship between higher education and political engagement. *Political Behavior 27*, 25–47.

Ho, J. (2003). *Youth and community: Engaging young people in philanthropy and service.* Battle Creek, MI: W. K. Kellogg Foundation.

Hodgkinson, V. A., and Weitzman, M. S. (1988a). *The charitable behavior of Americans: A national survey.* Washington, DC: Independent Sector.

Hodgkinson, V. A., and Weitzman, M. S. (1988b). *Giving and volunteering in the United States: Findings from a national survey.* Washington, DC: Independent Sector.

Hodgkinson, V. A., and Weitzman, M. S. (1990). *Giving and volunteering in the United States: Findings from a national survey.* Washington, DC: Independent Sector.

Hodgkinson, V. A., and Weitzman, M. S. (1992). *Giving and volunteering in the United States: Findings from a national survey.* Washington, DC: Independent Sector.

Hodgkinson, V. A., and Weitzman, M. S. (1994). *Giving and volunteering in the United States: Findings from a national survey.* Washington, DC: Independent Sector.

Hodgkinson, V. A., and Weitzman, M. S. (1996). *Giving and volunteering in the United States: Findings from a national survey.* Washington, DC: Independent Sector.

Hodgkinson, V. A., Weitzman, M. S., Noga, S. M., and Gorski, H. A. (1992). *Giving and volunteering in the United States: Findings from a national survey.* Washington, DC: Independent Sector.

Hoffman, M. K. (1977). Sex differences in empathy and related behaviors. *Psychological Bulletin, 84*(4), 712–722.

Hoge, D. R., and Yang, F. (1994). Determinants of religious giving in American denominations: Data from two nationwide surveys. *Review of Religious Research, 36*, 123–148.

Hogg, M. A. (1987). Social identity and group cohesiveness. In J. C. Turner *and others* (Eds.), *Rediscovering the social group: A self-categorization theory* (pp. 89–116). Oxford, England: Basil Blackwell.

Hollander, H. (1990). A social exchange approach to voluntary cooperation. *American Economic Review, 80*(5), 1157–1167.

Houston, D. J. (2006). "Walking the walk" of public service motivation: Public employees and charitable gifts of time, blood, and money. *Journal of Public Administration Research and Theory, 16*, 67–86.

Hunt, M. (1990). *The compassionate beast.* New York: William Morrow.

Hunt, S. D., and Morgan, R. M. (1994). The commitment-trust theory of relationship marketing. *Journal of Marketing, 58*(3), 20–38.

Hunter, C. S., Enid, B. J., and Boger, C. (1999). A study of the relationship between alumni and giving and selected characteristics of alumni donors of Livingstone College, NC. *Journal of Black Studies, 29*, 523–539.

Israel, A. C. (1978). Some thoughts on the correspondence between saying and doing. *Journal of Applied Behavior Analysis, 11*, 271–276.

Independent Sector (2011). *Vision*. Retrieved January 1, 2011, from http://www.independent sector.org/mission_and_values.

Jackson E. F., Bachmeier, M. D., Wood, J. R., and Craft, E. A. (1995). Volunteering and charitable giving: Do religious and associational ties promote helping behavior? *Nonprofit and Voluntary Sector Quarterly, 24,* 59–78.

Jackson, J. M., and Latané, B. (1981). Strength and number of solicitors and the urge toward altruism. *Personality and Social Psychology Bulletin, 7,* 415–422.

James, R. N., III. (2010, May/June). Barriers to bequest giving, *Advancing philanthropy,* 12–13.

Jencks, C., and Riesman, D. (1967). Negroes and their colleges. In C. Jencks and D. Riesman, (Eds.). *The Academic Revolution.* Chicago: University of Chicago Press.

Jha, P. K., Yadav, K. P., and Kuman, U. (1997). Gender difference and religio-cultural variation in altruistic behavior. *Indian Journal of Psychometry & Education, 28,* 105–108.

Jones, A. M., and Posnett, J. W. (1991). Charitable donations by UK households: Evidence from the family expenditure survey. *Applied Economics, 23,* 343–351.

Jones, L. (1982). The black churches in historical perspectives. *The Crisis, 89*(9), 402–406.

Joulfaian, D. (2000). Estate taxes and charitable bequests by the wealthy. Working Paper No. 7663. Cambridge, MA: National Bureau of Economic Research.

Journal of Blacks in Higher Education (1996). *Johnnetta Cole's resounding triumph: A wake-up call for HBCUs.* 13: 18–19.

Kamas, L., Preston, A., and Baum, S. (2008). Altruism in individual and joint-giving decisions: What's gender got to do with it? *Feminist Economics, 14,* 23–50.

Kang, C.-H. (2005, February). An exploration on individual giving and volunteering in Korea. Paper presented at a colloquium of the University of Pennsylvania School of Social Work, Philadelphia, PA.

Kaplan, A. E., and Hayes, J. (1993). What we know about women as donors. In A. J. Von Schlegell and J. M. Fisher (Eds.), *Women as donors, women as philanthropists.* New Directions for Philanthropic Fundraising (Number 2). San Francisco: Jossey-Bass.

Karoff, H. P. (Ed.). (2004). *Just money: A critique of contemporary American philanthropy.* Boston: TPI Editions.

Kelley, B. M, (1974). *Yale: A history.* New Haven: Yale University Press.

Kelly, K. (1991). *Fund raising and public relations: A critical analysis.* Hillsdale, NJ: Erlbaum.

Kelly, K. (1998). *Effective fund-raising management.* Mahwah, NJ: Erlbaum.

Kelly, K. (2002). The state of fund-raising theory and research. In M. J. Worth (Ed.), *New strategies for educational fund raising* (pp. 39–55). Westport, CT: American Council on Education/Praeger.

Kerns, J. R. (1986, June). Two-year college alumni programs into the 1990s. Paper presented at the National Workshop on Two-Year College Programs. Washington, DC: Junior and Community College Institute. (ED 277 435)

Keyt J. C., Yavas, U., and Riecken, G. (2002). Comparing donor segments to a cause-based charity: The case of the American Lung Association. *Journal of Nonprofit & Public Sector Marketing, 10,* 117–134.

Kimball, L. (1981). Interview by Marcia Goodson, United Negro College Fund Oral History Collection, Columbia University Oral History Collection, New York, NY.

Kingma, B. (1989). An accurate measurement of the crowd-out effect, income effect and price effect for charitable contributions. *Journal of Political Economy, 97,* 1197–1207.

Kohlberg, L. (1985). *The psychology of moral development.* San Francisco: Harper & Row.

Kotler, P. K. (1997). *Marketing management: Analysis, planning, implementation, and control.* Upper Saddle River, NJ: Prentice Hall.

Labaree, D. F. (1997). Public goods, private goods: The American struggle over educational goals. *American Educational Research Journal, 34*(1), 39–81.

Lerner, M. J. (1975). The justice motive of social behavior. *Journal of Social Issues, 31,* 1–20.

Leslie, L. L., and Ramey, G. (1988). Donor behavior and voluntary support of higher education institutions. *Journal of Higher Education, 59*(2), 115–132.

Levy, N. (2006). Against philanthropy, individual and corporate. In D. Elliott (Ed.), *The kindness of strangers: Philanthropy and higher education* (pp. 159–170). Lanham, MD: Rowman & Littlefield.

Lewis, D. (1994). *W.E.B. DuBois: Biography of a race, 1868–1919.* New York: Henry Holt.

Lincoln, E. E., and Mamiya, L. H. (1990). *The black church in the African American experience.* Durham, NC: Duke University Press.

Lindhal, W. E. (2009). *Principles of fundraising: Theory and practice.* Sudbury, MA: Jones & Bartlett.

Lindahl, W., and Winship, C. (1992). Predictive models for annual fundraising and major gift fundraising. *Nonprofit Management and Leadership, 3,* 43–64.

Lopez-Rivera, M. (2010, June 7). Updates on capital campaigns at 43 colleges and universities. *The Chronicle of Higher Education.* Retrieved on September 21, 2010, from http://chronicle.com/article/Updates-on-Capital-Campaigns/65807/.

Loseke, D. R. (1997). The whole spirit of modern philanthropy: The construction of the idea of charity, 1912–1992. *Social Problems, 44*(4), 425–444.

Lovitts, B. E. (2001). *Leaving the ivory tower: The causes and consequences of departure from doctoral study.* Lanham, MD: Rowman & Littlefield.

Lynch, H. G. (1980). The young alumnus: An enduring strength. In V. Carter and P. A. Alberger (Eds.), *Building your alumni programs: The best of CASE Currents.* Washington, DC: Council for the Advancement and Support of Education, (ED 192 697).

Lyons, M., and Nivison-Smith, I. (2006). Religion and giving in Australia. *Australian Journal of Social Issues, 41,* 419–436.

Lyons, M., and Passey, A. (2005). *Giving Australia: Research on philanthropy in Australia.* Sydney: University of Technology.

Mael, F., and Ashforth, B. E. (1992). Alumni and their alma mater: A partial test of the reformulated model of organizational identification. *Journal of Organizational Behavior, 13*(2), 103–123.

Marks, R. (1980). Legitimating industrial capitalism: Philanthropy and individual difference. In R. F. Arnove (Ed.), *Philanthropy and cultural imperialism: The foundations at home and abroad* (pp. 87–122). Bloomington: Indiana University Press.

Marr, K. A., Mullin, C. H., and Siegfried, J. J. (2005). Undergraduate financial aid and subsequent alumni giving behavior. *Quarterly Review of Economics and Finance, 45,* 123–143.

Martin, M. W. (1994). *Virtuous giving: Philanthropy, voluntary service, and caring.* Bloomington: Indiana University Press.

Marx, J. D. (2000). Women and human services giving. *Social Work, 45,* 27–38.

Massy, W. F. (1990). *Endowment: Perspective, policies, and management.* Washington, DC: Association of Governing Boards of Universities and Colleges.

Matsunaga, Y. (2006). To give or not to give, to volunteer or not to volunteer—that is the question. Evidence on Japanese philanthropic behavior revealed by the JGS-2005 data set.

Mays, B. (1987). Interview by Marcia Goodson, United Negro College Fund Oral History Collection, Columbia University Oral History Collection, New York, NY.

McClelland, R., and Kokoski, M. F. (1994). Econometric issues in the analysis of charitable giving. *Public Finance Quarterly, 22,* 498–517.

McGoldrick, W. P., and Robell, P. A. (2002). Campaigning in the new century. In M. J. Worth (Ed.), *New strategies for educational fund raising* (pp. 129–151). Westport, CT: Praeger.

McKenna, R. (1991). *Relationship marketing.* Reading, MA: Addison-Wesley.

Meer, J. (2008, November). *The habit of giving.* Working Paper. Stanford University.

Meier, S. (2007). Do women behave less or more prosocially than men? Evidence from two field experiments. *Public Finance Review, 35,* 215–232.

Mertens, S. (1998). Nonprofit organizations and social economy: Variations on a same theme. Paper presented at the Third International Conference of the International Society for Third Sector Research, Geneva, Switzerland.

Mesch, D. J., Rooney, P. M., Steinberg, K. W., and Denton, B. (2006). The effects of race, gender, and marital status on giving and volunteering in Indiana. *Nonprofit and Voluntary Sector Quarterly, 35,* 565–587.

Meuth, E. F. (1992). Corporate philanthropy in American higher education: An investigation of attitudes towards giving. Unpublished Ed.D. dissertation, University of Akron.

Midlarsky, E. (1971). Helping under stress: The effects of competence, dependency, visibility and fatalism. *Journal of Personality, 41,* 305–327.

Miley, W. (1980). Self-awareness and altruism. *Psychological Record, 30,* 3–8.

Miller, M. T., and Casebeer, A. L. (1990). Donor characteristics of college of education alumni: Examining undergraduate involvement. (ED 323836)

Miller, D. T. (1977). Personal deserving versus justice for others: An exploration of the justice motive. *Journal of Experimental Social Psychology, 13*(1), 1–13.

Miller, T. (2010). The context for development work in student affairs. *New Directions for Student Services* (Volume 130, pp. 3–8. DOI 10.1002/ss.355.

Monks, J. (2003). Patterns of giving to one's alma mater among young graduates from selective institutions. *Economics of Education Review, 22*(2), 121–130.

Moore, B. S., and Eisenberg, N. (1984). The development of altruism. *Annals of Child Development, 1,* 107–174.

Morison, S. E. (1986). *Three centuries of Harvard, 1636–1936*. Cambridge, MA: Harvard University Press.

Morphew, C., and Hartley, M. (2006). Mission statements: A thematic analysis of rhetoric across institutional type. *Journal of Higher Education, 77*(3), 456–471.

Mosser, J. W. (1993). Predicating alumni/ae gift giving behavior: A structural equation model approach. Unpublished doctoral dissertation, University of Michigan, Ann Arbor. (ED 355 883)

Mottino, F., and Miller, E. D. (2005). *Pathways for change: Philanthropy among African American, Asian American and Latino donors in the New York metropolitan region*. New York: Center on Philanthropy and Civil Society, City University of New York.

Mount, J. (1996). Why donors give. *Nonprofit management and leadership, 7*(1), 3–14.

Mulnix, M. W., Bowden, R. G., and López, E. E. (2002). A brief examination of institutional advancement activities at Hispanic-serving institutions. *Journal of Hispanic Higher Education, 1*, 174–190.

Musick, M., and Wilson, J. (2007). *Volunteers: A social profile*. Bloomington: Indiana University Press.

Nakada, L. H. (1993). Student interns: Cultivating the next generation of advancement professionals. In B. T. Todd (Ed.), *Student advancement programs: Shaping tomorrow's leaders today*. Washington, DC: Council for the Advancement and Support of Education.

Nasaw, D. (2006). *Carnegie*. New York: Penguin Group.

National Association of College and University Business Officers (2009). NACUBO-Commonfund Study of Endowments. Retrieved January 22, 2010 from http://www .nacubo.org/Research/NACUBO_Endowment_Study.html.

National Philanthropic Trust. (n.d.). *A chronological history of philanthropy in America*. Retrieved March 22, 2011, from http://74.52.60.18/~npt/index.php?page=quotes.

Nayman, R. L., Gianneschi, H. R., and Mandel, J. M. (1993). Turning students into alumni donors. In M. C. Terrell and J. A. Gold (Eds.), *New roles in educational fundraising and institutional advancement* (Volume 63, pp. 85–94). San Francisco: Jossey-Bass.

Nettles, M. T., and Millett, C. M. (2006). *Three magic letters: Getting to PhD*. Baltimore: Johns Hopkins University Press.

New England's First Fruits. (1643/2004). In D. F. Burlingame (Ed.), *Philanthropy in America: A comprehensive historical encyclopedia* (Volume 3, pp. 568–569). Santa Barbara, CA: ABC-CLIO.

Noonan, K., and Rosqueta, K. (2008). *"I'm not a Rockefeller": 33 high net worth philanthropists discuss their approach to giving*. Philadelphia: Center for High Impact Philanthropy, University of Pennsylvania.

Oates, B. (2004). *Unleashing youth potential: Understanding and growing youth participation in philanthropy and volunteerism*. Montreal: McGill University.

Okunade A. (1996). Graduate school alumni donations to academic funds: Microdata evidence. *American Journal of Economics and Sociology, 55*, 213–229.

Okunade, A., and Justice, S. (1991). Micropanel estimates of the life-cycle hypothesis with respect to alumni donations. In *Proceedings of the business and economics statistical section of the American Statistical Association* (pp. 298–305). Alexandria, VA: American Statistical Association.

Okunade, A., Wunnava, P. V., and Walsh, R., Jr. (1994). Charitable giving of alumni: Micro-data evidence from a large public university. *American Journal of Economics and Sociology, 53*, 73–84.

Olson, D.V.A., and Caddell, D. (1994). Generous congregations, generous givers: Congregational contexts that stimulate individual giving. *Review of Religious Research, 36,* 168–180.

Opinion Research Corporation (1990). "Survey Shows Differences in Blacks Giving." *Nonprofit Times* 3,19.

Palfrey, T. R., and Prisbrey, J. E. (1996). Altruism, reputation and noise in linear public goods experiments. *Journal of Public Economics, 61,* 409–427.

Palfrey, T. R., and Prisbrey, J. E. (1997). Anomalous behavior in public goods experiments: How much and why? *American Economic Review, 87*(5), 829–846.

Parsons, P. H. (2004). *Women's philanthropy: Motivations for giving.* Unpublished doctoral dissertation. Retrieved September 1, 2006, from ProQuest Doctoral Dissertations. AAT 3155889, http://www.proquest.com/.

Paton, G. J. (1986). Microeconomic perspectives applied to development planning and management. In J. A. Dunn (Ed.), *New directions for institutional research: Enhancing the management of fund raising* (Volume 51, pp. 17–37). San Francisco: Jossey-Bass.

Paton, R. (1991). The social economy: Value-based organizations in the wider society. In J. Batsleer and others (Eds.), *Issues in voluntary and nonprofit management.* Workingham, UK: Addison-Wesley.

Penney, S. W., and Rose, B. B. (2001). *Dollars for dreams: Student affairs staff as fundraisers.* Washington, DC: NASPA Press.

Pettey, J. G. (2002). *Cultivating diversity in fundraising.* San Francisco: Jossey-Bass.

Pezzullo, T. R., and Brittingham, B. E. (1993). Characteristics of donors. In J. M. Worth (Ed.), *Educational fund raising: Principles and practice.* Phoenix: Oryx Press.

Pharoah, C., and Tanner, S. (1997). Trends in charitable giving. *Fiscal Studies, 18,* 427–433.

Pickett, W. L. (1986). Fund raising effectiveness and donor motivation. In A. W. Rowland (Ed.), *Handbook of institutional advancement.* San Francisco: Jossey-Bass.

Piliavin, J. A., and Charng, H. (1990). Altruism: A review of recent theory and research. *Annual Review of Sociology, 16,* 27–65.

Piliavin, J. A., Dovidio, J. F., Gaertner, S. L., and Clark, R. D. (1981). *Emergency intervention.* New York: Academic Press.

Piper, G., and Schnepf, S. V. (2008). Gender differences in charitable giving in Great Britain. *Voluntas: International Journal of Voluntary and Nonprofit Organizations, 19*(2), 103–124.

Purpura, M. (1980). Building the alumni habit. In V. Carter and P. A. Alberger (Eds.), *Building your alumni programs: The best of CASE Currents.* Washington, DC: Council for the Advancement and Support of Education. (ED 192 697)

Ramos, H.A.J. (1999). Latino philanthropy: Expanding U.S. models of giving and civic participation. *Cultures of caring: Philanthropy in diverse American communities.* Washington, DC: Council on Foundations.

Ravitch, D. (2010). *The death and life of the great American school system: How testing and choice are undermining education.* New York: Basic Books.

Reece, W. S., and Zieschang, K. D. (1985). Consistent estimation of the impact of tax deductibility on the level of charitable contributions. *Econometrica, 53,* 271–293.

Reed, P. B., and Selbee, L. K. (2002). Is there a distinctive pattern of values associated with giving and volunteering? The Canadian case. Paper presented at the 32nd ARNOVA conference, Montreal, QC.

Regnerus, M. D., Smith, C., and Sikkink, D. (1998). Who gives to the poor? The influence of religious tradition and political location on the personal generosity of Americans toward the poor. *Journal for the Scientific Study of Religion, 37,* 481–493.

Ribar, D. C., and Wilhelm, M. O. (2002). Altruistic and joy-of-giving motivations in charitable behavior. *Journal of Political Economy, 110*(2), 425–457.

Rimmerman, C. A. (1997). The *new citizenship: Unconventional politics, activism, and service.* Boulder, CO: Westview.

Rissmeyer, P. A. (2010). Student affairs and alumni relations. *New Directions for Student Services* (Volume 130, pp. 19–29). DOI: 10.1002/ss.357.

Ritterband, P., and Wechsler, H. S. (1994). *Jewish learning in American universities: The first century.* Bloomington: Indiana University Press.

Roberts, R. D. (1984). A positive model of private charity and public transfers. *Journal of Political Economy, 92*(1), 136–148.

Rooney, P., Brown, E., and Mesch, D. (2007). Who decides in giving to education? A study of charitable giving by married couples. *International Journal of Educational Advancement, 7*(3), 229–242.

Rooney, P., Steinberg, K., and Schervish, P.G. (2001). A methodological comparison of giving surveys: Indiana as a test case. *Nonprofit and Voluntary Sector Quarterly, 30,* 551–568.

Rosenhan, D. L. (1970). The natural socialization of altruistic autonomy. In J. Macauley and L. Berkowitz (Eds.), *Altruism and help behavior* (pp. 251–268). New York: Academic Press.

Rosenhan, D. L. (1978). Toward resolving the altruism paradox: Affect self-reinforcement and cognition. In L. Wispe (Ed.), *Altruism, sympathy, and helping.* New York: Academic Press.

Rudolph, F. J. (1962). *The American college and university: A history.* New York: Vintage Books.

Rushton, J. P. (1975). Generosity in children: Immediate and long-term effects of modeling, preaching, and moral judgment. *Journal of Personality and Social Psychology, 31,* 459–466.

Rushton, J. P. (1982). Social learning theory and the development of prosocial behavior. In N. Eisenburg (Ed.), *The development of prosocial behavior.* New York: Academic Press.

Sansone, C., and Harackiewicz, J. M. (2000). Looking beyond rewards: The problem and promise of intrinsic motivation. In C. Sansone and J. M. Harackiewicz (Eds.), *Intrinsic and extrinsic motivation: The search for optimal motivation and performance.* San Diego: Academic Press.

Sapp, R. E., and Kimball, P. K. (2002). Planned giving. In M. J. Worth (Ed.), *New strategies for educational fund raising.* Westport, CT: American Council on Education/Praeger.

Sargeant, A., and McKenzie, J. (1998). *A lifetime of giving: An analysis of donor lifetime value.* Research Report No. 4. Kings Hill, Kent, England: Charities Aid Foundation.

Schervish, P. G. (1993). Taking giving seriously. In P. Dent (Ed.), *Taking giving seriously.* Indianapolis: Indiana University Center on Philanthropy.

Schervish, P. G. (1997). Inclination, obligation, and association: What we know and what we need to learn about donor motivation. In D. F. Burlingame (Ed.). *Critical issues in fundraising.* San Francisco: Wiley.

Schervish, P. G. (2003). *Inclination, obligation, and association: What we know and what we need to learn about donor motivations.* Boston: Association for the Study of Higher Education.

Schervish, P. G., and Havens, J. J. (1997). Social participation and charitable giving: A multivariate analysis. *Voluntas: International Journal of Voluntary and Nonprofit Organizations, 8*(3), 235–260.

Schervish, P. G., and Havens, J. J. (1998). Money and magnanimity: New findings on the distribution of income, wealth, and philanthropy. *Nonprofit Management and Leadership, 8*(4), 421–434.

Schiff, J. (1990). *Charitable giving and government policy: An economic analysis.* New York: Greenwood Press.

Schlegelmilch, B. B., Diamantopoulos, A., and Love, A. (1997). Characteristics affecting charitable donations: Empirical evidence from Britain. *Journal of Marketing Practice: Applied Marketing Science, 3,* 14–28.

Schroeder, D. A., Penner, L. A., Dovidio, J. F., and Piliavin, J. A. (1995). *The psychology of helping and altruism: Problems and puzzles.* New York: McGraw-Hill.

Schroeder, F. W. (2002). The annual giving program. In M. J. Worth (Ed.), *New strategies for educational fund raising.* Westport, CT: American Council on Education/Praeger.

Schuppert, G. F. (1991). State, market, third sector: Problems of organizational choice in the delivery of public services. *Nonprofit and Voluntary Sector Quarterly, 20,* 125–136.

Schwartz, S. H., and Ben-David, T. (1976). Responsibility and helping in an emergency: Effects of blame, ability and denial of responsibility. *Sociometry, 39,* 406–415.

Shanley, M. G. (1985). Student, faculty and staff involvement in institutional advancement: University of South Carolina. *Carolina View, 1*, 40–43. (ED 272 133)

Shaw-Hardy, S., and Taylor, M. A. (2010). *Women and philanthropy: Boldly shaping a better world.* San Francisco: Jossey-Bass.

Shiva, V. (2003). *Globalisation and its fall out.* Retrieved June 23, 2010, from http://www.globenet3.org/Articles/Article_Globalization_Shiva.shtml.

Shoemaker, B. (2008). The emerging distinction between theology and religion at nineteenth-century Harvard University. *Harvard Theological Review, 101*(3–4), 417–430.

Simon, G., and Ernst, F. (1996). Does social exchange increase voluntary cooperation? *Kyklos, 49*(4), 541–555.

Smith, B., Shue, S., Vest, J. L., and Villarreal, J. (1999). *Philanthropy in communities of color.* Bloomington: Indiana University Press.

Smith, C. L., Gelfand, D. M., Hartmann, D. P., and Partlow, M.E.P. (1979). Children's casual attributions regarding help giving. *Child Development, 50,* 203–210.

Smith, D. (1991). Four sectors or five? Retaining the member-benefit sector. *Nonprofit and Voluntary Sector Quarterly, 20*(2), 137–150.

Sokolowski S. W. (1996). Show me the way to the next worthy deed: Towards a microstructural theory of volunteering and giving. *Voluntas, 7,* 259–278.

Sowell, T. (1972). *Black education: Myths and tragedies.* New York: David McKay.

Spaeth, J. L., and Greeley, A. M. (1970). *Recent alumni and higher education: A survey of college graduates.* New York: McGraw-Hill.

Spears, A. M. (2001). Structuring planned gifts. In K. E. Dove (Ed.), *Conducting a successful fundraising program* (pp. 210–241). San Francisco: Jossey-Bass.

Spring, J. (2004). *Deculturalization and the struggle for inequality: A brief history of the education of dominated cultures in the United States.* Boston: McGraw-Hill.

Steinberg, R. (1987). Voluntary donations and public expenditures in a Federalist system. *American Economic Review, 77*(1), 24–36.

Steinberg, R., and Wilhelm, M. (2003a). Giving: The next generation—parental effects on donations. Working Paper No. CPNS 21. Indianapolis: Indiana University Center on Philanthropy.

Steinberg, R., and Wilhelm, M. (2003b). Tracking giving across generations. *New Directions for Philanthropic Fundraising* (Volume 42, pp. 71–82). San Francisco: Jossey-Bass.

Steinberg, R., and Wilhelm, M. (2005). Religion and secular giving, by race and ethnicity. *New Directions for Philanthropic Fundraising* (Volume 48, pp. 57–66). San Francisco: Jossey-Bass.

Steinberg, R., Wilhelm, M., Rooney, P., and Brown, E. (2002). Inheritance and charitable donations (Working paper). Indianapolis: Indiana University Center on Philanthropy.

Sugden, R. (1982). On the economics of philanthropy. *Economic Journal, Royal Economic Society, 92*(366), pp. 41–50.

Sugden, R. (1984). Reciprocity: The supply of public goods through voluntary contributions. *Economic Journal, 94*(376), 772–787.

Sweet, J. H. (1996). *Uncovering philanthropy in the African American community: A bibliographic approach.* Paper presented at the Silver Anniversary Conference of the Association for Research on Nonprofit Organizations and Voluntary Action, New York, NY.

Taylor, A. L., and Martin, J. C., Jr. (1993, May). *Predicating alumni giving at a public research university.* Paper presented at the Annual Forum of the Association for Institutional Research, Chicago, IL. (ED 360 929)

Terrell, M., Gold, J., and Renick, J. C. (1993). Student affairs professionals as fund-raisers: An untapped resource. *NASPA Journal, 30*(3), 190–195.

Thelin, J. (2004). *A history of American higher education.* Baltimore: Johns Hopkins University Press.

Thompson, J. D., Katz, S., and Briechle, P. (2010). A high level annual fund without an annual ask. *International Journal of Educational Advancement, 9*(4), 273–280.

Thorndike, E. L. (1912). *Education.* New York: Macmillan.

Thorndike, E. L. (1929). Investigating curriculum: The psychologists dissect the course of study. *Journal of Adult Education, 1*: 41–48.

Tiehen, L. (2001). Tax policy and charitable contributions of money. *National Tax Journal, 54,* 707–723.

Todd, S. J., and Lawson, R. W. (1999). Towards a better understanding of the financial donor: An examination of donor behavior in terms of value structure and demographics. *International Journal of Nonprofit and Voluntary Sector Marketing, 4,* 235–244.

Trent, W. J., Jr. (1981). Interview by Marcia Goodson, United Negro College Fund Oral History Collection, Columbia University Oral History Collection, New York, NY.

Tsunoda, K. (2010). Asian American giving to US higher education. *International Journal of Educational Advancement, 10*(1), 2–23.

Tsunoda, K. (2011). *Unraveling the myths of Chinese American giving: Exploring donor motivations and effective fundraising strategies for U.S. higher education.* Unpublished Ph.D. dissertation, University of Maryland.

van Fleet, J. (2010). Critiquing corporate philanthropy. Unpublished working paper. University of Maryland.

Van Nostrand, I. (1999). Young alumni programming. In J. A. Feudo (Ed.), *Alumni relations: A newcomer's guide to success.* Washington, DC: Council for the Advancement and Support of Education.

Van Slyke, D. M., and Brooks, A. C. (2005). Why do people give? New evidence and strategies for nonprofit managers. *American Review of Public Administration, 35*(3), 199–222.

Van Til, J. (1988). *Mapping the third sector: Volunteerism in a changing social economy.* New York: Foundation Center.

Verba, S., Schlozman, K. L., and Brady, H. E. (1995). *Voice and equality: Civic volunteerism in American politics.* Cambridge, UK: Cambridge University Press.

Vesterlund, L. (2004). Why do people give? In W. E. Powell and R. W. Steinberg (Eds.), *The nonprofit sector: A research handbook* (pp. 568–590). New Haven: Yale University Press.

Walton, A. (2000). Rethinking boundaries: The history of women, philanthropy, and higher education, *History of Higher Education Annual, 20.*

Walton, A. (2005). *Women and philanthropy in education.* Bloomington: Indiana University Press.

Walton, A. (2008). Philanthropy in higher education: Past and present. In A. Walton and M. Gasman (Eds.), *Philanthropy, volunteerism and fundraising in higher education.* Boston: Pearson.

Walton, A., and Gasman, M. (Eds.). (2008). *Philanthropy, volunteerism, and fundraising.* Upper Saddle River, NJ: Pearson.

Warr, P. G. (1982). Pareto optimal redistribution and private charity. *Journal of Public Economics, 19,* 131–138.

Warr, P. G. (1983). The private provision of a public good is independent of the distribution of income. *Economics Letters, 13,* 207–211.

Warren, P. E., and Walker, I. (1991). Empathy, effectiveness and donations to charity: Social psychology's contribution. *British Journal of Social Psychology, 30,* 325–337.

Washington, B. T. (1910/2008). How to help most with money. In A. Walton and M. Gasman (Eds.), *Philanthropy, volunteerism and fundraising in higher education.* Boston: Pearson.

Watkins, W. (2001). *White architects of black education.* New York: Teachers College Press.

Weyant, J. M. (1984). Applying social psychology to induce charitable donations. *Journal of Applied Social Psychology, 14,* 441–447.

White House Council of Economic Advisors. (2000, November 25). *Philanthropy in the American economy: A report by the Council of Economic Advisors.* Available at http://clinton4.nara.gov/media/philanthropy.pdf.

Wiepking, P., and Maas, I. (2006). Resources that make you generous: Effects of human, financial, and social resources on charitable giving. Working Paper. Amsterdam: Department of Philanthropy, Vrije Universiteit, Amsterdam.

Wilhelm, M. O., Brown, E., Rooney, P. M., and Steinberg, R. S. (2006). The intergenerational transmission of generosity. Working Paper. Indianapolis: Indiana University–Purdue University Indianapolis.

Wilson, E. O. (1975). *Sociobiology: The new synthesis.* Cambridge, MA: Harvard University Press.

Worth, M. (2002). *New strategies for educational fundraising.* New York: Praeger.

Worth, M. (2010). *Leading the campaign: Advancing colleges and universities.* Plymouth, UK: Rowman & Littlefield.

Wunnava, P. V., and Lauze, M. A. (2001). Alumni giving at a small liberal arts college: Evidence from consistent and occasional donors. *Economics of Education Review, 20,* 533–543.

Wylie, P. B., and Sammis, J. (2008). Does data mining really work for higher education fundraising? A study of the results of predictive models built for 5 higher education institutions. Washington, DC: CASE. Retrieved March 22, 2011, from http://www.case.org/Documents/Books/29502/Does_Data_Mining_Really_Work.pdf.

Yamauchi, N., and Yokoyama, S. (2005). What determines individual giving and volunteering in Japan? An econometric analysis using the 2002 national survey data. Paper presented at the 34th ARNOVA Conference, Washington, DC.

Yates, E. L. (2001). Capital campaigns. *Black Issues in Higher Education, 18*(10), 18–25.

Yavas, U., Riecken, G., and Parameswaran, R. (1981). Personality, organization-specific attitude, and socio-economic correlates of charity giving behavior. *Journal of the Academy of Marketing Science, 9,* 52–65.

Yen, S. T. (2002). An econometric analysis of household donations in the USA. *Applied Economics Letters, 9,* 837–841.

Young, P. S., and Fischer, N. M. (1996, May). Identifying undergraduate and post-college characteristics that may affect alumni giving. Paper presented at the Annual Forum of the Association for Institutional Research, Albuquerque, NM. (ED 397 748).

Supplemental Bibliography

Abbe, M. A. (2000). The roots of minority giving. *Currents, 26*(6), 36–40.

Adamson, R. (2006). Indigenous peoples and philanthropy: Colonialism by other means? *Alliance, 11,* 40–1.

Adetimirin, A. (2008). Crisis in black nonprofits. *Network Journal, 15*(9), 10.

Aguirre, A., and Min, L. (2005). *Familia, fé y comunidad: Giving and volunteering among Hispanics in Silicon Valley.* San Jose, CA: Silicon Valley Community Foundation.

Ajzen, I. (1991). The theory of planned behavior. *Organizational Behavior and Human Decision Processes, 50,* 179–211.

Ambler, M. (1994). Indian giving: The new philanthropy in Indian country. *Tribal College Journal, 6*(3), 14–23.

Anderson, B. E. (1993). *Philanthropy and charitable giving among large black business owners.* Indianapolis, IN: Association of Black Foundation Executives.

Andreoni, J., and Petrie, R. (2007). Beauty, gender, and stereotypes: Evidence from laboratory experiments. *Journal of Economic Psychology, 29*(2008), 73–93.

Andreoni, J., and Vesterlund, L. (2001). Which is the fair sex? Gender differences in altruism. *Quarterly Journal of Economics, 116*(1), 293–312.

Anft, M. (2007, October 18). Inching to the top: Nonprofit managers who are minorities search for a quicker way up the ladder. *Chronicle of Philanthropy, 20*(1), 4.

A. P. Smith Manufacturing Company, Plaintiff-Respondent v. *Ruth F. Barlow, William B. Campbell, William M. Brenn, Eugene M. Smith and Joseph P. Halpin, Individually and as Representatives of the Holders of the Preferred and Common Shares of the A. P. Smith Manufacturing Company, Defendants-Appellants, and Theodore D. Parsons, Attorney-General of New Jersey, Defendant-Respondent,* 13 N.J. 145; 98 A.2d 581; 1953 N.J. C.F.R. (1953).

Arca, P. (1994). Why diversity? *Advancing Philanthropy, 2,* 11–13.

Arminio, J., Clinton, L. F., and Harpster, G. (2010). Fundraising for student affairs at comprehensive institutions. *New Directions for Student Services* (Volume 130, pp. 31–45). San Francisco: Jossey-Bass.

Asian American Federation. (2001). *A new heritage of giving: Philanthropy in Asian America.* New York: Asian American Federation of New York.

Asian Pacific American Community Fund. (1996). *Asian Pacific American nonprofits: Perceptions and realities.* San Francisco: Asian Pacific American Community Fund.

Asimov, N. (1990, June 25). White males dominate foundation boards: Watchdog group surveyed 75 boards across U.S.—5 in Bay Area. *San Francisco Chronicle,* A5.

Bakewell, T. (2006). Mega campaigns for colleges and universities: Achieving success. *International Journal of Educational Advancement, 6*(3), 253–257.

Bakker, F.G.A., Groenewegen, P., and Den Hond, F. (2005). A Bibliometric Analysis of 30 Years of Research and Theory on Corporate Social Responsibility and Corporate Social Performance. *Business Society, 44,* 283–317.

Baron, B., and Bozorgmehr, M. (2001). *Philanthropy among Middle Eastern Americans and their historical traditions of giving.* New York: Center for the Study of Philanthropy, City University of New York.

Barrett, R., and Ware, M. E. (2001). *Planned giving essentials: A step-by-step guide to success.* Gaithersburg, MD: Aspen Publishers.

Barrick, M. R., and Mount, M. K. (1996). Effects of impression management and self-deception on the predictive validity of personality constructs. *Journal of Applied Psychology, 81*(3), 261–272.

Bartlett, C. V. (2003, December 16). Beyond numbers and compliance: Valuing cultural diversity in national nonprofit capacity-building organizations. *ENHANCE: The Newsletter of the Alliance for Nonprofit Management, 1,* 1–10.

Bartolini, W. F. (2001). Using a communication perspective to manage diversity in the development office. *New Directions for Philanthropic Fundraising, 2001*(34). 47–75.

Baugh, L. L. (Ed). (2005). Black philanthropy: From words to action. *Proceedings of the Fourth National Conference on Black Philanthropy.* Washington, DC: National Center for Black Philanthropy.

Bekkers, R. (2003). Trust, accreditation, and philanthropy in the Netherlands. *Nonprofit and Voluntary Sector Quarterly, 32,* 596–615.

Bekkers, R. (2007). Measuring altruistic behavior in surveys: The all-or-nothing dictator game. *Survey Research Methods, 1*(3), 139–144.

Ben-Ner, A., Kong, F., and Putterman, L. (2004). Share and share alike? Intelligence, socialization, personality, and gender-pairing as determinants of giving. *Journal of Economic Psychology 25,* 581–589.

Bergstrom, T., Blume, L., and Varian, H. (1985). On the private provision of public goods. *Journal of Public Economics, 29,* 25–49.

Berkshire, J. C. (2008). Missing persons: Why do so few black men hold top leadership jobs at nonprofit groups? *Chronicle of Philanthropy, 20*(23), 8–10.

Berry, M. L., and Chao, J. (2001). *Engaging diverse communities for and through philanthropy.* Washington, DC: Forum of Regional Associations of Grantmakers.

Bianchi, A. (2006). Rethinking corporate philanthropy: Exploiting core competencies is only half the story. *Stanford Social Innovation Review,* 12–13.

Bishop, M., and Green, M. (2008). *Philanthrocapitalism: How the rich can save the world.* New York: Bloomsbury Press.

Block, D. S. (1997). Virtue out of necessity: A study of Jewish philanthropy in the United States, 1890–1918. Unpublished Ph.D. dissertation, University of Pennsylvania.

Blumenstyk, G. (2010, March 7). Financial affairs: Why the endowment-spending debate matters now more than ever. *Chronicle of Higher Education*. Retrieved March 10, 2010, from http://chronicle.com/article/Why-the-Endowment-Debate/64527/.

Bremmer, R. H. (1960). *American philanthropy*. Chicago: University of Chicago Press.

Bremner, R. H. (1996). *Giving: Charity and philanthropy in history*. New Brunswick, NJ: Transaction Publishers.

Brockett, L. P. (1864). *The philanthropic results of the war in America*. New York: Sheldon & Co.

Brown, E. (2006). Married couples' charitable giving: Who and why. In M. A. Taylor and S. Shaw-Hardy (Eds.), *The transformative power of women's philanthropy* (pp. 69–80), San Francisco: Wiley.

Brown, M., and Rooney, P. (2008). *Men, women, X and Y: Generational and gender differences in motivations for giving*. Proceedings from The Center on Philanthropy at Indiana University 20th Annual Symposium, Indianapolis, IN.

Brown, W.A. (2002). Inclusive governance practices in nonprofit organizations and implications for practice. *Nonprofit Management & Leadership, 12*(4), 369–385.

Bruch, H., and Walter, F. (2005). The keys to rethinking corporate philanthropy. *MIT Sloan Management Review, 47*(1), 49–55.

Brudney, V., and Ferrell, A. (2002). Corporate charitable giving. *University of Chicago Law Review, 69*(3), 1191–1218.

Bryson, E., and Parsons, S. (2003). *What foundation boards are saying about diversity*. Washington, DC: Council on Foundations.

Buchanan, A. (1987). Justice and charity. In D. Elliott (Ed.), *The kindness of strangers* (pp. 139–158). New York: Rowman & Littlefield Publishers.

Burbridge, L. C. (1995). *Status of African Americans in grant making institutions*. Indianapolis: Indiana University Center on Philanthropy.

Burbridge, L. C., Diaz, W. A., Odendahl, T., and Shaw, A. (2002). *The meaning and impact of board and staff diversity in the philanthropic field: Findings from a national study*. San Francisco: Joint Affinity Groups.

Campoamor, D., Diaz, W. A., and Ramos, H.A.J. (Eds.). (1999). *Nuevos senderos: Reflections on Hispanics and philanthropy*. Houston: Arte Publico Press.

Carnegie, A. (1889, June). Wealth. *North American Review, 148,* 653–664.

Carroll, A. (1999). Corporate social responsibility: Evolution of a definitional construct. *Business Society, 38*(3), 268–295.

Carson, E. (1987a). *Black philanthropic activity past and present: A 200-year tradition continues*. Washington DC: Joint Center for Political Studies.

Carson, E. (1987b). *Pulling yourself up by your bootstraps: The evolution of black philanthropic activity*. Washington DC: Joint Center for Political Studies.

Carson, E. (1990). *Black volunteers as givers and fundraisers*. New York: Center for the Study of Philanthropy, City University of New York.

Carson, E. (1994). Diversity and equity among foundation grant makers. *Nonprofit Management and Leadership, 4*(3), 331–344.

Carson, E. (2001). Giving strength: Understanding philanthropy in the black community. *Philanthropy Matters, 2, 4.*

Carson, E. (2005). Black philanthropy's past, present and future. *New Directions for Philanthropic Fundraising* (Volume 48, pp. 5–12). San Francisco: Jossey-Bass.

Carver, J., and Carver, M. M. (1997). *Making diversity meaningful in the boardroom.* San Francisco: Jossey-Bass.

Chandler, L. C. (2005). Beyond political correctness: Discover the benefits of board diversity. *Association Management, 57*(1), 29–30.

Chao, J. (2001). Asian-American philanthropy: Acculturation and charitable vehicles. *ARNOVA, 1*(1), 57–79.

Chavers, G. D. (2001). The role of planned giving professionals: Serving nonprofit organizations and their donors. *New Directions in Philanthropic Fundraising* (Volume 30). San Francisco: Jossey-Bass.

Clift, E. (Ed.). (2005). *Women, philanthropy and social change.* Medford, MA: Tufts University Press.

Clinton, W. J. (2007). *Giving: How each of us can change the world.* New York: Knopf.

Clohesy, S. J. (2004). *Donor circles: Launching and leveraging shared giving.* San Francisco: Women's Funding Network.

Clotfelter, C. T. (2003a). Alumni giving to elite private colleges and universities. *Economics of Education Review, 22*(2), 109–120.

Clotfelter, C. T. (2003b). Who are the alumni donors? Giving by two generations of alumni from selective colleges. *Nonprofit Management & Leadership, 12*(2), 119–138.

Cook, W. B. (2008). Fund raising and the college presidency in an era of uncertainty: From 1975 to the present. In A. Walton and others (Eds.), *Philanthropy, volunteerism and fundraising in higher education* (pp. 626–645). Boston: Pearson.

Cook, W. B. (1997). Surveying the major gifts literature: Observations and reflections. *Nonprofit Leadership and Management, 7*(3), 333–347.

Cornelius, M., and Lew, S. (2009). What about the next generation of leaders of color? Advancing multicultural leadership. *Nonprofit World, 27*(4), 24–26.

Cortés, M. (1999). Do Hispanic nonprofits foster Hispanic philanthropy? *New Directions for Philanthropic Fundraising, 1999*(24), 31–24.

Council for Financial Aid to Education. (1973). *Volunteerism, tax reform, and higher education.* New York: Council for Financial Aid to Education.

Council on Foundations. (1993). *Inclusive practices in philanthropy: Report and commentary of the Council on Foundations Task Force on Inclusiveness and Staff.* Washington, DC: Council on Foundations.

Cunningham, B. M., and Cochi-Ficano, C. K. (2002). The determinants of donative revenue flows from alumni of higher education: An empirical inquiry. *Journal of Human Resources, 37*(3), 540–569.

Curti, M. (1958). American philanthropy and the national character. *American Quarterly, 10*(4), 420–437.

Daley, J. M. (2002). An action guide for nonprofit board diversity. *Journal of Community Practice, 10*(1), 33–54.

Delgado, L. T., Orellana-Damacela, L. E., and Zanoni, M. J. (2001). *Chicago philanthropy: A profile of the grant making profession.* Chicago: Loyola University Chicago.

Drezner, N. D. (2010a). *Adding science to the art of fundraising: The power of using data in fundraising strategy.* Association of Fundraising Professionals Research Council. Retrieved December 1, 2010, from http://www.afpnet.org/ResourceCenter/ArticleDetail.cfm?Item Number=4572.

Drezner, N. D. (2010b). Fundraising in a time of economic downturn. Theory, practice, and implications: An editorial call to action. *International Journal of Educational Advancement, 9*(4), 191–195.

D'Souza, H. (1975). External influences on the development of education policy in British tropical Africa from 1923 to 1939. *African Studies Review, 18*(2), 35–43.

Dufwenberg, M., and Muren, A. (2006). Generosity, anonymity, gender. *Journal of Economic Behavior & Organization, 61*, 42–49.

Dysart, N. M. (1989). Alumni-in-resident: Programs for students. In C. H. Webb (Ed.), *Handbook for alumni administration.* New York: Macmillan.

Eagly, A. H., and Koenig, A. M. (2006). Social role theory of sex differences and similarities: Implication for prosocial behavior. In K. Dindia and D. J. Canary (Eds.), *Sex differences and similarities in communication* (pp. 161–177). Mahwah, NJ: Erlbaum.

Eckel, C. C., and Grossman, P. J. (2008). Differences in the economics decisions of men and women: Experimental evidence. In C. R. Plott and V. L. Smith (Eds.), *Handbook of experimental economics results* (Volume 1, pp. 509–518). Linacre House, UK: North-Holland Publishers.

Ehrenberg, R. G., and Smith, C. L. (2003). The sources and uses of annual giving at selective private research universities and liberal arts colleges. *Economics of Education Review, 22*(3), 223–235.

Eisenberg, N., and Lennon, R. (1983). Sex differences in empathy and related capacities. *Psychological Bulletin, 94,* 100–131.

Enay, S. (2009). Big island: GIRL POWER. *Hawaii Business, 54*(8), 18.

Erdle, S., Sansom, M., Cole, M. R., and Heapy, N. (1992). Sex differences in personality correlates of helping behavior. *Personality & Individual Differences, 13*, 931–936.

Eveland, V. B., and Crutchfield, T. N. (2007). Understanding why people do not give: Strategic funding concerns for AIDS-related nonprofits. *International Journal of Nonprofit and Voluntary Sector Marketing, 12*, 1–12.

Ewin, A., and Wollock, J. (1996). *Survey of grant giving by American Indian foundations and organizations.* Lumberton, NC: Native Americans in Philanthropy.

Expanding Nonprofit Inclusiveness Initiative. (2003). *Inside inclusiveness: Race, ethnicity and nonprofit organizations.* Denver: Denver Foundation.

Fairfax, J. E. (1995). Black philanthropy: Its heritage and its future. In W. Ilchman and C. Hamilton (Eds.), *Cultures of giving II: How heritage, gender, wealth, and values influence philanthropy.* New Directions in Philanthropic Fundraising (Volume 8, pp. 9–21). San Francisco: Jossey-Bass.

Frank, R. (1996). Motivation, cognition, and charitable giving. In J. B. Schneewind (Ed.), *Giving: Western ideas of philanthropy* (pp. 130–152). Indianapolis: Indiana University Press.

Frey, B. S., and Meier, S. (2005). Selfish and indoctrinated economists? *European Journal of Law and Economics, 19,* 165–171.

Friedman, L. J., and McGarvie, M. D. (Eds.). (2003). *Charity, philanthropy, and civility in American history.* Bloomington: Indiana University Press.

Gachter, S., and Fehr, E. (1996). Does social exchange increase voluntary cooperation? *Kyklos, 49*(4), 541–555.

Gallegos, H. E., and O'Neill, M. (Eds.). (1991). Hispanics *and the nonprofit sector.* New York: Foundation Center.

Gallo, P. J., and Hubschman, B. (2003). The relationships between alumni participation and motivation on financial giving. Paper presented at an annual meeting of the American Educational Research Association, Chicago, IL. Retrieved September 15, 2005, from http://search.ebscohost.com/login.aspx?direct=trueanddb=ericandAN=ED477447 andloginpage=Login.aspandsite=ehost-live.

Garriga, E., and Mele, D. (2004). Corporate social responsibility theories: Mapping the territory. *Journal of Business Ethics, 53,* 51–71.

Gary, T., and Kohner, M. (2002). *Inspired philanthropy: Creating a giving plan.* Berkeley, CA: Chardon Press.

Gasman, M. (2004). Sisters in service: African-American sororities and philanthropic support of education. In A. Walton (Ed.), *Stewards, scholars, and patrons: Studies in the history of women, philanthropy, and education.* Bloomington: Indiana University Press.

Gasman, M. (2005). The role of faculty in fundraising at black colleges: What is it and what can it become? *International Journal of Educational Advancement, 5*(2), 171–179.

Ginsberg, A., and Gasman, M. (Eds.). (2007). *Gender and educational philanthropy: New perspectives on funding, collaboration and assessment.* New York: Palgrave Macmillan.

Ginsberg, L. D. (1990). *Women and the work of benevolence: Morality, politics, and class in the nineteenth-century United States.* New Haven: Yale University Press.

Giroux, H. A. (1998, October). Education Incorporated? *Educational Leadership,* 12–17.

Gitin, M. (2001). Beyond representation: Building diverse board leadership teams. *New Directions for Philanthropic Fundraising* (Volume 34, pp. 77–100). San Francisco: Jossey-Bass.

Gittell, R., and Tebaldi, E. (2006). Charitable giving: Factors influencing giving in the U.S. States. *Nonprofit and Voluntary Sector Quarterly, 35,* 721–736.

Goranson, R., and Berkowitz, L. (1966). Reciprocity and responsibility reactions to prior help. *Journal of Personality and Social Psychology, 3*(2), 227–232.

Gouldner, A. W. (1960). The norm of reciprocity: A preliminary statement. *American Sociological Review, 25,* 161–178.

Greene, M. P. (2007). Beyond diversity and multiculturalism: Towards the development of anti-racist institutions and leaders. *Journal for Nonprofit Management, 11*, 9–17.

Greene, S. G., Hall, H., and Stehle, V. (1994, September 20). The nonprofit world's diversity dilemma. *Chronicle of Philanthropy, 6*, 26–29.

Gutiérrez, J. A. (n.d.). *Report on Latinos and philanthropy in the United States*. New York: Center on Philanthropy and Civil Society, City University of New York.

Hall, H. (1999, June 3). Black philanthropy: A focus on careers and building endowments. *Chronicle of Philanthropy, 11*, 31–32.

Hall, M. R. (2002). Fundraising and public relations: A comparison of programme concepts and characteristics. *International Journal of Nonprofit and Voluntary Sector Marketing, 7*(4), 368–382.

Hallgarth, S., and Capek, M. E. (1995). *Who benefits, who decides? An agenda for improving philanthropy: The case for women and girls*. New York: National Council for Research on Women.

Hamilton, C. H., and Ilchman, W. R. (1995). *Cultures of giving II: How heritage, gender, wealth and values influence philanthropy*. San Francisco: Jossey-Bass.

Harrison, W. H., Michell, S. K., and Peterson, S. P. (1995). Alumni donations and colleges' development expenditures: Does spending matter? *American Journal of Economics and Sociology, 54*(4), 397–412.

Havens, J. (1995). Passing it on: The generational transmission of wealth and financial care. In P. G. Schervish, V. A. Hodgkinson, and M. Gates (Eds.), *Care and community in modern society: Passing on the tradition of service to future generations* (pp. 109–133). San Francisco: Jossey-Bass.

Havens, J. J., O'Herlihy, M. A., and Schervish, P. G. (2006). Charitable giving: How much, by whom, to what, and how? In W. W. Powell and R. Steinberg (Eds.), *The nonprofit sector: A research handbook* (2nd ed., pp. 542–567). New Haven: Yale University Press.

Hispanics in Philanthropy. (2004). *Reflection, action, and expansion: Analysis of the challenges and opportunities for the development of emerging Latino community in Boulder County, Colorado*. San Francisco: Hispanics in Philanthropy.

Holloman, D., Gasman, M., and Anderson-Thompkins, S. (2003). Motivations for philanthropic giving in the African American church: Implications for black college fundraising. *Journal of Research on Christian Education, 12*(2), 137–169.

Homans, G. C. (1958). Social behavior as exchange. *American Journal of Sociology, 63*(6), 597–606.

Hoyt, J. E. (2004). Understanding alumni giving: Theory and predictors of donor status. Paper presented at the 44th Annual Forum of the Association for Institutional Research, Boston, MA. Retrieved November 10, 2010, from http://www.eric.ed.gov/ERICWeb Portal/search/detailmini.jsp?_nfpb=true&_&ERICExtSearch_SearchValue_0=ED4909 96&ERICExtSearch_SearchType_0=no&accno=ED490996.

Huges, P., and Luksetich, W. (2008). Income volatility and wealth: The effect on charitable giving. *Nonprofit and Voluntary Sector Quarterly, 37*, 264–280.

Hunt, E. (2003). *African-American philanthropy: A legacy of giving*. New York: Twenty-First Century Foundation.

Hunt, E., and Maurrasse, D. (2004). *Time, talent and treasure: A study of black philanthropy.* New York: Twenty-First Century Foundation.

Israel, D. K. (2007). Charitable donations: Evidence of demand for environmental protection? *International Advances in Economic Research, 13,* 171–182.

Jackson, R. M. (Ed). (1998). *At the crossroads: Proceedings of the first national conference on black philanthropy.* Oakton, VA: Corporation for Philanthropy.

Jackson, R. M. (Ed). (2000a). Moving the agenda forward. *Proceedings of the second national conference on black philanthropy.* Washington, DC: National Center for Black Philanthropy.

Jackson, R. M. (Ed.). (2000b). *Philanthropy and the black church: New problems, new visions.* Vienna, VA: Corporation for Philanthropy.

Jackson, T. D. (2001). Young African Americans: A new generation of giving behavior. *International Journal of Nonprofit and Voluntary Sector Marketing, 6*(3), 243.

Jones, A. L. (1996). Philanthropy in the African American experience. In J. B. Schneewind (Ed.), *Giving: Western ideas.* Bloomington: Indiana University Press.

Jones, L. (2009, October 14). Christianity and charity. *New Statesman.* Retrieved November 1, 2010, from http://www.newstatesman.com/print/200904270002.

Joseph, J. A. (1995). *Remaking America: How the benevolent traditions of many cultures are transforming our national life.* San Francisco: Jossey-Bass.

Joslyn, H. (2007). Image vs. reality: The nonprofit's world of inclusion is still a dream for many organizations. *Chronicle of Philanthropy, 20*(1), 3.

Kaminski, A. R. (2003). Women as donors. In H. A. Rosso and E. R. Tempel (Eds.), *Achieving excellence in fund raising* (pp. 200–214). San Francisco: Jossey-Bass.

Karl, B. D., and Katz, S. N. (1981). *The American private philanthropic foundation and the public sphere: 1890–1930*: Kluwer Academic Publishers.

Kasper, G., Ramos, H.A.J., and Walker, C. J. (2004). Making the case for diversity in philanthropy. *Foundation News & Commentary, 45*(6), 26–35.

Kottasz, R. (2004). Differences in the donor behavior characteristics of young affluent males and females: Empirical evidence from Britain. *Voluntas, 15,* 181–203.

Landry, C., and others. (2006). Toward an understanding of the economics of charity: Evidence from a field experiment. *Quarterly Journal of Economics, 121,* 747–782.

Lee, R. (1990). *Guide to Chinese American philanthropy and charitable giving patterns.* San Rafael, CA: Pathway Press.

Levy, R. (1999). *Give and take: A candid account of corporate philanthropy.* Boston: Harvard Business School Press.

Light, I., Kwuon, I. J., and Zhong, D. (1990). Korean rotating credit associations in Los Angeles. *Amerasia, 16*(1), 35–54.

Lindsey, K. R. (2006). *Racial, ethnic, and tribal philanthropy: A scan of the landscape.* Washington, DC: Forum of Regional Associations of Grantmakers.

Lipman, H. (2002). Minority homeowners give more to charity than whites, study finds. *Chronicle of Philanthropy, 14*(6), 14.

List, J. A. (2004). Young, selfish, and male: Field evidence of social preferences. *Economic Journal, 114,* 121–149.

McCarthy, K. D. (Ed.). (1990). *Lady bountiful revisited: Women, philanthropy and power.* New Brunswick, NJ: Rutgers University Press.

McCarthy, K. D. (2001). *Women, philanthropy, and civil society.* Bloomington: Indiana University Press.

McKinley-Floyd, L. A. (1998). The impact of values on the selection of philanthropic clubs by elite African American women: An historical perspective. *Psychology & Marketing, 15*(2), 145.

Midlarsky, E., and Hannah, M. E. (1989). The generous elderly: Naturalistic studies of donations across the life span. *Psychology and Aging, 4,* 346–351.

Miller, J. L., Fletcher, K., and Abzug, R. (1999). *Perspectives on nonprofit board diversity.* Washington, DC: National Center for Nonprofit Boards.

Minnesota Council on Foundations. (2005). *Working towards diversity III: A progress report on strategies for inclusiveness among Minnesota grant makers.* Minneapolis: Minnesota Council on Foundations.

Moody, M. (1994). Pass it on: Serial reciprocity as a principle of philanthropy. *Essays on Philanthropy, 13.* Bloomington: Indiana University Center on Philanthropy.

Moore, J. (1993, November 16). Nonprofits trail government and business in ethnic and racial diversity. *Chronicle of Philanthropy, 6,* 27–30.

Munson, L. (2008). Endowment reform: Why universities should share their vast wealth and in the process make higher education more affordable. Working paper. Center for College Affordability and Productivity. Retrieved November 15, 2010, from http://www .centerforcollegeaffordability.org/uploads/Miller_Munson_corrected.pdf.

Murphy, T. B. (2000). Financial and psychological determinants of donors' capacity to give. In E. R. Tempel and D. Burlingame (Eds.), *Understanding the needs of donors: The supply side of charitable giving.* New Directions in Philanthropic Fundraising (Volume 29, pp. 33–51). San Francisco: Jossey-Bass.

Musick, M. A., and Wilson, J. (2007). *Volunteers: A social profile.* Bloomington: Indiana University Press.

Navarro, P. (1988). Why do corporations give to charity? *Journal of Business, 61*(1), 65–93.

Nelson, J., and Prescott, D. (2005). *Partnering for success: Business perspectives on multistakeholder partnership.* Geneva: World Economic Forum.

"New coalition promotes ethnic philanthropy in New York." (2001). *CPA Journal, 71*(12), 18.

Newman, D. (2002). *Opening doors: Pathways to diverse donors.* San Francisco: Jossey-Bass.

Newman, R. H. (1995). Perception of factors relating to gender differences in philanthropy. Unpublished doctoral dissertation, University of San Francisco. Retrieved June 27, 2006, from ProQuest Digital Dissertations. AAT 9532669.

Ostrander, S. A., and Schervish, P. G. (1990). *Giving and getting: Philanthropy as a social relation.* Boston: Association for the Study of Higher Education.

Ostrower, F. (2007). *Nonprofit governance in the United States: Findings on performance and accountability from the first national representative study.* Washington, DC: Urban Institute.

Paupard, J. (1995). *American Indians and philanthropy: A summary report of the December 1994 Forum.* St. Paul: American Indian Research and Policy Institute.

Payton, R. (1988). *Philanthropy: Voluntary action for the public good.* New York: American Council on Education/Macmillan.

Payton, R. (2008). A dialogue between the head and the heart. In A. Walton and others (Eds.), *Philanthropy, volunteerism and fundraising in higher education* (pp. 53–55). Boston: Pearson.

Peck, K. C. (2002). Philanthropy and American Indians: Ancient traditions meet modern giving. In R. E. Foyal (Ed.), *Fundraising in Diverse Cultural and Giving Environments.* New Directions for Philanthropic Fundraising (Volume 37, pp. 55–63). San Francisco: Jossey-Bass.

Perry, S. (2006). Tapping Hispanic philanthropy. *Chronicle of Philanthropy, 18*(24), 7–12.

Phipps, S. A., and Burton, P. S. (1998). What's mine is yours? The influence of male and female incomes on patterns of household expenditure. *Economica, 65,* 599–613.

Pomazal, R. J., and Jaccard, J. J. (1976). An informational approach to altruistic behavior. *Journal of Personality and Social Psychology, 33*(3), 317–326.

Poock, M. C., and Siegel, D. J. (2005). Benchmarking graduate student development practices. *International Journal of Educational Advancement, 6*(1), 11–19.

Prince, M. (1993). Women, men, and money styles. *Journal of Economic Psychology, 4,* 175–182.

Ramos, H.A.J., and Kasper, G. (2000). *Building a tradition of Latino philanthropy: Hispanics as donors, grantees, grant makers, and volunteers.* Los Angeles: Center on Philanthropy and Public Policy, University of Southern California.

Reed, M. (2005). *Strategic philanthropy: Assessing the needs of the Native philanthropic sector.* Fredericksburg, VA: First Nations Development Institute.

Rogers, P. C. (1999). African American traditions of giving and serving: A midwest perspective. *Nonprofit and Voluntary Sector Quarterly, 28*(3), 348.

Rogers, P. C. (Ed.). (2001). *Philanthropy in communities of color: Traditions and challenges.* Indianapolis: Association for Research on Nonprofit Organizations and Voluntary Action.

Romero, A. D. (1998). *Globalized Latinos: The opportunities and challenges of leadership. An address to the Hispanics in philanthropy board of directors.* Santo Domingo, Dominican Republic: Hispanics in Philanthropy.

Rooney, P., Mesch, D. J., Chin, W., and Steinberg, K. S. (2005). The effects of race, gender, and survey methodologies on giving in the US. *Economics Letters, 86,* 173–180.

Rose-Ackerman, S. (1996). Altruism, nonprofits, and economic theory. *Journal of Economic Literature, 34,* 701–728.

Rosenblatt, J.A.C., Alain, J., and McGown, L. (1986). A model to explain charitable donation: Health care consumer behavior. *Advances in Consumer Research, 13*(1), 235–239.

Royce, A. P., and Rodriguez, R. (1999). From personal charity to organized giving: Hispanic institutions and values of stewardship and philanthropy. In L. Wagner and A. F. Deck (Eds.), *Hispanic Philanthropy: Exploring the Factors That Influence Giving and Asking: New Directions for Philanthropic Fundraising.* New Directions for Philanthropic Fundraising (Volume 24, pp. 9–29). San Francisco: Jossey-Bass.

Rutledge, J. M. (1994). *Building board diversity.* Washington, DC: National Center for Nonprofit Boards.

Rutnik, T. A., and Bearman, J. (2005). *Giving together: A national scan of giving circles and shared giving*. Washington, DC: Forum of Regional Associations of Grantmakers.

Samuels, D. (1995). Philanthropic correctness: The failure of American foundations. *New Republic, 213*(12/13), 28–36.

Sandmann, L. R., and Weerts, D. J. (2008). Reshaping institutional boundaries to accommodate an engagement agenda. *Innovative Higher Education, 33*(3), 181–196.

Schervish, P. G. (2005). Major donors, major motives: The people and the purpose behind major gifts. In L. Wagner and T. L. Seiler (Eds.), *Reprising Timeless Topics*. New Directions for Philanthropic Fundraising (Volume 47, pp. 59–87). San Francisco: Jossey-Bass.

Schervish, P. G., and Havens, J. (1995). Do the poor pay more: Is the U-shaped curve correct? *Nonprofit and Voluntary Sector Quarterly, 24,* 79–90.

Schneider, J. A. (2003). Small, minority-based nonprofits in the information age. *Nonprofit Management & Leadership, 13*(4), 383.

Sears, J. B. (1922/1990). *Philanthropy in the history of American higher education*. New Brunswick, NJ: Transaction Publishers.

Seifert, B., Morris, S. A., and Bartkus, B. R. (2003). Comparing big givers and small givers: Financial correlates of corporate philanthropy. *Journal of Business Ethics, 45*(3), 195–211.

Sharpe, R., Sr. (1999). *Planned giving simplified: The gift, the giver, and the gift planner*. Alexandria, VA: Association of Fundraising Professionals.

Shaw, S., and Taylor, M. (1995). *Reinventing fundraising: Realizing the potential of women's philanthropy*. San Francisco: Jossey-Bass.

Shaw-Hardy, S. (2000). *Creating a women's giving circle*. Rochester, MI: Women's Philanthropy Institute.

Shrestha, N., McKinley-Floyd, L., and Gillespie, M. (2008). Promoting philanthropy in the black community: A macroscopic exploration. *Journal of Macromarketing, 28*(1), 91.

Sidberry, T. B. (2002). Building diversity in organizations. *Nonprofit Quarterly, 8*(2), 28–33.

Siegel, E. (2002). Prospect research and research management. In M. J. Worth (Ed.), *New strategies for educational fund raising* (pp. 283–296). Westport, CT: Praeger.

Skoe, E.E.A., and others. (2002). The influences of sex and gender-role identity on moral cognition and prosocial personality traits. *Sex Roles: A Journal of Research, 46*(9–10), 295–309.

Smith, B., Shue, S., and Villarreal, J. (1999). *Asian and Hispanic philanthropy*. San Francisco: Institute for Nonprofit Organization Management.

Smith, C. (2003). The new corporate philanthropy. In *Harvard Business Review on Corporate Responsibility* (pp. 157–187). Boston: Harvard Business School Publishing.

Smith, J. R., and McSweeney, A. Charitable giving: The effectiveness of a revised theory of planned behavior model in predicting donating intentions and behavior. *Journal of Community and Applied Social Psychology, 17,* 363–386.

Spann, J., and Springer, C. (1993). *The value of difference: Enhancing philanthropy through inclusiveness in governance, staffing and grant making*. Washington, DC: Council on Foundations.

Spears, A. M. (2001). Developing and marketing a planned giving program. In K. E. Dove (Ed.), *Conducting a successful fundraising program* (pp. 199–209). San Francisco: Jossey-Bass.

Stately, J. E. (2002). Walking softly across the dialogue of religion, spirituality, and the Native American experience of giving. In D. F. Burlingame (Ed.), *Taking Fundraising Seriously: The Spirit of Faith and Philanthropy: New Directions for Philanthropic Fundraising*. New Directions for Philanthropic Fundraising (Volume 35, pp. 79–96). San Francisco: Jossey-Bass.

Stephens, C. R. (2005). Professionalism in black philanthropy: We have a chance to get it right. In P. Rooney and L. Sherman (Eds.), *Exploring Black Philanthropy*. New Directions for Philanthropic Fundraising (Volume 48, pp. 13–19). San Francisco: Jossey-Bass.

Stewart, D. M., Rock Kane, P., and Scruggs, L. (2002). Education and training. In L. Salamon (Ed.), *The state of nonprofit America* (pp. 107–148). Washington, DC: Brookings Institution.

Taylor, A. L., and Martin, C., Jr. (1995). Characteristics of alumni donors and nondonors at a research public university. *Research in Higher Education, 36*(3), 283–302.

Taylor, M. A., and Shaw-Hardy, S. (Eds.). (2005). *The transformative power of women's philanthropy*. New Directions for Philanthropic Fundraising (Number. 50). San Francisco: Jossey-Bass.

Tempel, E. R., and Smith, L. (2007). Leadership diversity: The nonprofit sector has a spotty record on advancement. *NonProfit Times, 21*(5), 14–15.

Thomas, J. A., and Smart, J. (1995). *The relationship between personal and social growth and involvement in college and subsequent alumni giving*, Paper presented at an annual forum of the Association for Institutional Research, San Diego, CA.

Tipsord Todd, B. (Ed.). (1993). *Student advancement programs: Shaping tomorrow's alumni leaders today*. Washington, DC: CASE Books.

Tobin, G. A. (2001). *The transition of communal values and behavior in Jewish philanthropy*. San Francisco: Institute for Jewish & Community Research.

Turner, S., Meserve, L., and Bowen, W. (2001). Winning and giving: Football results and alumni giving at selective private colleges and universities. *Social Science Quarterly, 82*(4), 812–826.

Van Slyke, D. M., Ashley, S., and Johnson, J. L. (2007). Nonprofit performance, fundraising effectiveness, and strategies for engaging African Americans in philanthropy. *American Review of Public Administration, 37*(3), 278.

Varadarajan, P. R., and Menon, A. (1988). Cause-related marketing: A coalignment of marketing strategy and corporate philanthropy. *Journal of Marketing, 52*(3), 58–74.

Von Schlegell, A. J., and Fisher, J. M. (1993). *Women as donors, women as philanthropists*. San Francisco: Jossey-Bass.

Wagner, L., and Patrick, R. J. (2004). Achieving diversity among fundraising professionals. *New Directions for Philanthropic Fundraising,* (Volume 43, pp. 63–70). San Francisco: Jossey-Bass.

"Walsh again tilts with Rockefeller." (1915, May 23). *New York Times*.

Walton, A. (2008). Philanthropy in higher education: Past and present. In A. Walton and others (Eds.), *Philanthropy, volunteerism and fundraising in higher education* (pp. 3–12). Boston: Pearson.

Wedgeworth, R. (2000). Donor relations as public relations: Toward a philosophy of fundraising. *Library Trends, 48*(3), 530–539.

Weerts, D. J. (2000). Outreach as a critical link to state support for research universities. *Journal of Higher Education Outreach and Engagement, 6*(1), 49–56.

Weerts, D. J. (2005a). Facilitating knowledge flow in community-university partnerships. *Journal of Higher Education Outreach and Engagement, 10*(3), 23–38.

Weerts, D. J. (2005b). Validating institutional commitment to outreach: Listening to the voices of community partners. *Journal of Extension, 43*(5). Retrieved June 23, 2007, from http://www.joe.org/joe/2005october/a3.shtml.

Weerts, D. J. (2007a). Facilitating university engagement with schools. *Metropolitan Universities, 18*(4), 67–86.

Weerts, D. J. (2007b). Toward an engagement model of institutional advancement at public colleges and universities. *International Journal of Educational Advancement, 7*(2), 79–103.

Weerts, D. J., Cabrera, A. F., and Sanford, T., (2010). Beyond giving: Political advocacy and volunteer roles of college alumni. *Research in Higher Education, 51*(4), 346–365.

Weerts, D. J., and Ronca, J. M. (2006). Examining differences in state support for higher education: A comparative study of state appropriations for research universities. *Journal of Higher Education, 77*(6), 935–965.

Weerts, D. J., and Ronca, J. M. (2007). Profiles of supportive alumni: Donors, volunteers, and those who "do it all." *International Journal of Educational Advancement, 7*(1), 20–34.

Weerts, D. J., and Ronca, J. M. (2008). Characteristics of alumni donors who volunteer at their alma mater. *Research in Higher Education, 49*(3), 274–292.

Weerts, D. J., and Ronca, J. M. (2009). Using classification trees to predict alumni giving for higher education. *Education Economics, 17*(1), 95–122.

Weerts, D. J., and Sandmann, L. R. (2008). Building a two-way street: Challenges and opportunities for community engagement at research universities. *Review of Higher Education, 32*(1), 73–106.

White, D. E. (1998). *The art of planned giving: Understanding donors and the culture of giving.* New York: Wiley.

Whitehouse, L. (2003). Corporate social responsibility, Corporate citizenship and the global compact. *Global Social Policy, 3*(3), 299–318.

Whitehouse, L. (2006). Corporate social responsibility: Views from the frontline. *Journal of Business Ethics, 63*(3), 279–296.

Williamson, O. E. (1963). Managerial discretion and business behavior. *American Economic Review, 53*(5), 1032.

Winterich, K. P., Mittal, V., and Ross, W. T. (2009). Donation behavior toward in-groups and out-groups: The role of gender and moral identity. *Journal of Consumer Research, 36,* 199–214.

Winters, M. F. (1996). *Include me! Making the case for inclusiveness for private and family foundations.* Washington, DC: Council on Foundations.

W. K. Kellogg Foundation. (1999). *Emerging philanthropy in communities of color: A report on current trends.* Battle Creek, MI: W. K. Kellogg Foundation.

Women and Foundations/Corporate Philanthropy. (1990). *Far from done: The challenge of diversifying philanthropic leadership.* New York: Women and Foundations/Corporate Philanthropy.

Name Index

A

Adams, John Hurst, 32
Ahammer, I. M., 66
Albert, S., 54
Alperovitz, G., 81
American Association of Fundraising
    Counsel, 12
Anderson, E., 22, 23, 81, 83, 84
Anderson, J. D., 22, 81, 83
Anderson-Thompkins, S., 31, 34, 56, 62,
    77
Andreoni, J., 42, 44, 48, 51
Anft, M., 30
Apinunmahakul, A., 71
Arnove, R. F., 81, 82
Ascoli, P., 23
Ashcraft, R. F., 18
Ashforth, B. E., 54, 55, 56, 61, 62
Astin, A., 69
Atchley, R. C., 7, 53, 61, 63, 67
Avalos, J., 69
Avery, R., 14

B

Bachmeier, M. D., 50
Banks, J., 71
Bar-Tal, D., 59, 66
Baum, S., 42
Beaumont, E., 86
Beaz, B., 69
Becker, G. S., 50
Bekkers, R., 42, 60, 71, 72, 73

Belfield, C. R., 42
Ben-David, T., 58
Beney, A. P., 42
Bentley, R. J., 58, 59, 60
Bergstrom, T. C., 49
Berman, E., 81
Berry, M. L., 39
Bielfeld, W., 71
Billig, S., 86
Birkholz, J., 75, 77
Bjorhovde, P. O, 60, 68, 69
Blanchette, R., 61
Blau, P. M., 53
Blume, L., 49
Blumenfeld, W. S., 72
Boger, C., 56
Bolton, G. E., 42
Boverini, L., 52
Bowden, R. G., 37
Bradford, A., 21
Brady, H. E., 86
Brawley, J. P., 66
Bremner, R. H., 60
Briechle, P., 73
Brittingham, B. E., 2, 15, 56, 60, 61
Broce, T., 5, 60
Brooks, A. C., 71, 72
Brown, E., 14, 42, 43, 44, 68, 71, 72, 80
Brown-Kruse, J., 42
Bruggink, T. H., 56
Buchan, N., 42
Burgoyne, C. B., 44
Burnett, K., 2, 52

Kimball, L., 83
Kimball, P. K., 8
Kingma, B., 71
Kohlberg, L., 66
Kokoski, M. F., 71
Kotler, P. K., 52
Kuczynski, L., 60
Kuman, U., 43

L

Labaree, D. F., 80
Lankford, H., 43, 71
Lasher, W. F., 53
Latané, B., 42
Lauze, M. A., 44, 45, 72
Lawson, R. W., 72
Lerner, M. J., 57
Leslie, L. L., 26, 54, 56
Levy, N., 80, 81
Lewis, D., 23, 82, 83, 84
Lincoln, E. E., 31
Lindahl, W., 7, 53, 63, 67
Lipman, H., 30
Loession, B. A., 25
Lopez-Rivera, M., 11
Loseke, D. R., 79
Love, A., 72
Lovitts, B. E., 61
Lu, F., 36
Lynch, H. G., 67
Lyons, M., 42, 71

M

Maas, I., 72
Mael, F., 54, 55, 56, 61, 62
Mamiya, L. H., 31
Mandel, J. M., 61, 63, 67
Marks, R., 83
Marr, K. A., 73
Martin, J. C., Jr., 50, 51, 56
Marx, J. D., 72
Massy, W. F., 9, 10
Matsunaga, Y., 71
Mays, B., 83

McCarthy, S., 71
McClelland, R., 71
McGoldrick, W. P., 7, 8
McKenna, R., 52
McKenzie, J., 52, 53
Mead, M., 28
Meer, J., 67
Meier, S., 42
Mertens, S., 80
Mesch, D., 42, 43, 71
Mesch, D. J., 42, 43
Meuth, E. F., 18, 25
Miley, W., 66
Miller, D. T., 57, 70
Miller, E. D., 29
Miller, Linda, 24
Miller, M. T., 56
Millett, C. M., 61
Monks, J., 63, 67, 73, 74
Moore, B. S., 66
Morgan, R. M., 52
Morphew, C., 86
Moss, A., 23, 81, 84
Mosser, J. W., 56
Mottino, F., 29
Mount, J., 57
Mullin, C., 73
Mulnix, M. W., 37
Murray, J. P., 66
Musick, M., 43
Mussen, P. H., 58

N

Nakada, L. H., 67
Nasaw, D., 23
Nash, R., 19, 22, 24, 82, 84
Nayman, R. L., 61, 63, 67
Nettles, M. T., 61
Newman, C., 71
Nissan, L. G., 58, 59, 60
Nivison-Smith, I., 42, 71
Noga, S. M., 43
Noonan, K., 52

Subject Index

A

African American philanthropy, 29–35, 40

Altruism, 80; debates about, 48; impure, 51; multiperson, 50; public good versus pure, 48–49

Alumni donors, 2, 10–11; Asian American, 38–39; cultural differences of, 26; endowment gifts from, 9; engaging current students to be, 86; experiences as students of, 69–70; gender differences of, 44–45; giving to historically black institutions by contemporary, 34–35; history of, 5; motivations of, 47, 53; organizational identification by, 54–57; predictors of giving by, 56–57; systematic solicitation of, 24–26; views of, 88; women, 45

American higher education: British support for, 18–19; colonial colleges, 19–20

American Indian philanthropy, 39

Annual funds, 6–7

Annuities, 9

Asian American philanthropy, 37–39

Association of Fundraising Professionals, 77

Atchley's theory, 7, 63

B

Bequests, 2–3, 9; "Last Will and Testament of Miss Sophia Smith," 21; tax deductions for, 13

Bill and Melinda Gates Foundation, 13

Billionaire Boy's Club, 84

Black colleges/universities: alumni gifts to, 35; contemporary alumni donations to, 34–35; creation of, 22–23; fundraising by, 32–34; handling of fundraising by, 5; HBCUs (historically black colleges and universities), 86; history of giving to, 83; support by white donors of, 22, 84; support through church of, 31–32

Black donors, 29–35

Boston College, 43

Brawley's principle, 66–67

British support for American higher education, 18–19

Brown v. *Board of Education*, 82

C

Campaigns, 7–8, 11–12, 25

Capitalism, 79–80, 81–82

Center for High Impact Philanthropy, 52

Center on Nonprofits and Philanthropy, 77

Center on Philanthropy, 14

Center on Philanthropy and Civil Society, 31

Charitable gift annuities, 9

Charitable instruments/options, 8–9

Charitable lead trusts, 9

Charitable remainder trusts, 9

Children: modeling giving for, 59–60; motivations for giving of, 65–66

Chinese American philanthropy, 38

Chronicle of Philanthropy, 30

Citizenship, engaged, 86

Coalition for New Philanthropy, 29–30

About the Author

Noah D. Drezner is an assistant professor of higher education at the University of Maryland. His research interests include philanthropy and fundraising as they pertain to colleges and universities, including higher education's role in the cultivation of prosocial behaviors. His work has received two awards from the Council for the Advancement and Support of Education. He serves on the editorial board of the *International Journal of Educational Advancement* and the Association for Fundraising Professionals Research Council. His professional experience includes serving as a development officer at the University of Rochester's Office of College Advancement.

About the ASHE Higher Education Report Series

Since 1983, the ASHE (formerly ASHE-ERIC) Higher Education Report Series has been providing researchers, scholars, and practitioners with timely and substantive information on the critical issues facing higher education. Each monograph presents a definitive analysis of a higher education problem or issue, based on a thorough synthesis of significant literature and institutional experiences. Topics range from planning to diversity and multiculturalism, to performance indicators, to curricular innovations. The mission of the Series is to link the best of higher education research and practice to inform decision making and policy. The reports connect conventional wisdom with research and are designed to help busy individuals keep up with the higher education literature. Authors are scholars and practitioners in the academic community. Each report includes an executive summary, review of the pertinent literature, descriptions of effective educational practices, and a summary of key issues to keep in mind to improve educational policies and practice.

The Series is one of the most peer reviewed in higher education. A National Advisory Board made up of ASHE members reviews proposals. A National Review Board of ASHE scholars and practitioners reviews completed manuscripts. Six monographs are published each year and they are approximately 120 pages in length. The reports are widely disseminated through Jossey-Bass and John Wiley & Sons, and they are available online to subscribing institutions through Wiley InterScience (http://www.interscience.wiley.com).

Call for Proposals

The ASHE Higher Education Report Series is actively looking for proposals. We encourage you to contact one of the editors, Dr. Kelly Ward (kaward@wsu.edu) or Dr. Lisa Wolf-Wendel (lwolf@ku.edu), with your ideas.

Recent Titles

ORDER FORM SUBSCRIPTION AND SINGLE ISSUES

DISCOUNTED BACK ISSUES:

Use this form to receive 20% off all back issues of *ASHE Higher Education Report*.
All single issues priced at **$23.20** (normally $29.00)

TITLE	ISSUE NO.	ISBN

Call 888-378-2537 or see mailing instructions below. When calling, mention the promotional code JBNND to receive your discount. For a complete list of issues, please visit www.josseybass.com/go/aehe

SUBSCRIPTIONS: (1 YEAR, 6 ISSUES)

☐ New Order ☐ Renewal

U.S.	☐ Individual: $174	☐ Institutional: $265
CANADA/MEXICO	☐ Individual: $174	☐ Institutional: $325
ALL OTHERS	☐ Individual: $210	☐ Institutional: $376

Call 888-378-2537 or see mailing and pricing instructions below.
Online subscriptions are available at www.onlinelibrary.wiley.com

ORDER TOTALS:

Issue / Subscription Amount: $ _____

Shipping Amount: $ _____
(for single issues only – subscription prices include shipping)

Total Amount: $ _____

SHIPPING CHARGES:

First Item	$5.00
Each Add'l Item	$3.00

(No sales tax for U.S. subscriptions. Canadian residents, add GST for subscription orders. Individual rate subscriptions must be paid by personal check or credit card. Individual rate subscriptions may not be resold as library copies.)

BILLING & SHIPPING INFORMATION:

☐ **PAYMENT ENCLOSED:** *(U.S. check or money order only. All payments must be in U.S. dollars.)*

☐ **CREDIT CARD:** ☐ VISA ☐ MC ☐ AMEX

Card number _____ Exp. Date _____

Card Holder Name _____ Card Issue # _____

Signature _____ Day Phone _____

☐ **BILL ME:** *(U.S. institutional orders only. Purchase order required.)*

Purchase order # _____
Federal Tax ID 13559302 • GST 89102-8052

Name _____

Address _____

Phone _____ E-mail _____

Copy or detach page and send to: **John Wiley & Sons, PTSC, 5th Floor**
989 Market Street, San Francisco, CA 94103-1741

Order Form can also be faxed to: **888-481-2665**

PROMO JBNND

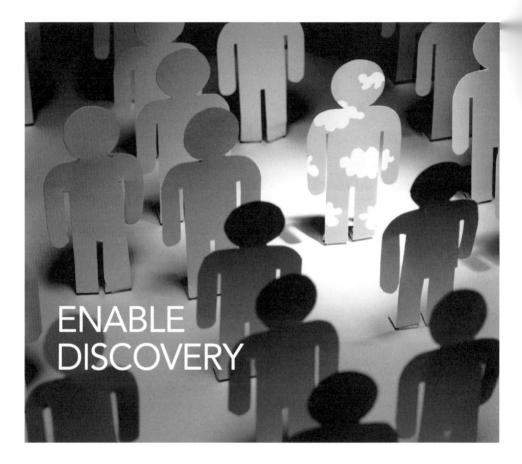

ENABLE
DISCOVERY

Introducing WILEY ONLINE LIBRARY

Wiley Online Library is the next-generation content platform founded on the latest technology and designed with extensive input from the global scholarly community. Wiley Online Library offers seamless integration of must-have content into a new, flexible, and easy-to-use research environment.

Featuring a streamlined interface, the new online service combines intuitive navigation, enhanced discoverability, an expanded range of functionalities, and a wide array of personalization options.

wileyonlinelibrary.com

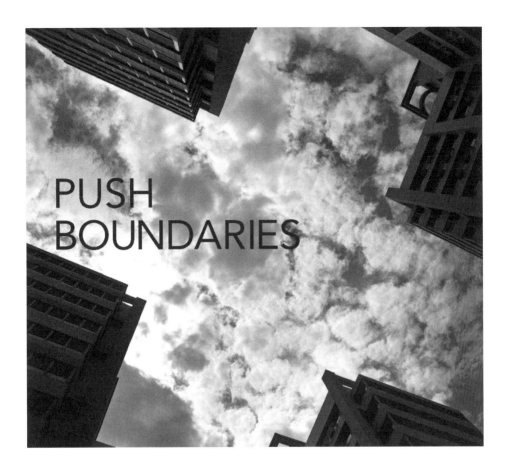